METHUEN'S OLD ENGLISH LIBRARY

FINNSBURH

Fragment and Episode

METHUEN'S OLD ENGLISH LIBRARY

General Editors

A. J. Bliss, Professor of Old and Middle English,
University College, Dublin

and

A. Brown, Professor of English, Monash University

Eodem metro conditum forte reperi fragmenti poëtici singulare folium, in codice MS. homiliarum *Semi-Saxonicarum* qui extat in Bibliotheca *Lambethana*. Fragmentum autem subsequitur.

* * * * * * * * * * * * * * *
* nar bẏnnað. [ȝeonȝ cẏninȝ.
Næfne hleoþrode ða heaþo
Ne ðir ne baȝað Eartun.
Ne heþþnaca ne fleoȝeð.
Ne heþ ðirre healle hoþnar ne
    bẏnnað.
Ac heþ roþþþenað.
Fuȝelar rinȝað.
Lẏlleð ȝnæȝhama.
Liuð puþu hlẏnneð.
Scẏlð rcefte oncpẏð.
Nu rcẏneð þer mona.
Faðol unðer polcnum.
Nu apirað pea-bæða.
De ðir ne folcer nið.
Fþemman pillað.
Ac on pacniȝeað nu.
Piȝenð mine.
Dabbað eoppe lanða.
Die ȝeaþ on ellen.
Pinþað on onþe.
Feraþ on moðe.
Da apar mæniȝ ȝolðhlaben
    ðeȝn.
Liẏnþe hine hir rpunþe.
Da to þupa eoþon.
Dpihtlice cempan.

Siȝeƿeþ anð Eaha.
Dẏna rpoþ ȝetuȝon.
Anð æt oþþum ðupum.
Opðlaf anð Liuþlaf.
Anð Denȝert rẏlf.
Dpeanf him on larte.
Da ȝẏt Liapulf.
Liuðere rtẏnoðe.
Dæt he rpa freolic feoþh.
Foþ·man riþe.
To ðæþe healle ðupum.
Dẏpẏta ne bæpan.
Nu hẏt niþa heapð.
Anẏ man polðe.
Ac he fpaȝn oþeþ eal.
Unðeapninȝa.
Deopmoð hæleþ.
Dþa ða ðupu heolðe.
Siȝeƿeþþ ir min Nama cpeþ he.
Ic eom recȝena leoð.
Þpecten piðe cuð.
Fæla ic peuna ȝebað.
Deopðþa hilða.
De ir ȝẏt heppitoð.
Spæþeþ ðu rẏlf to me.
Secean pẏlle.
Da pær on healle.
Fæl-rlihta ȝehlẏn.

Sceolðe Lelær boþð.
Lenumon hanða.
Banhelm beþrtan.
Bupuhðelu ðẏneðe.
Oð æt ðæþe ȝuðe.
Liapulf * ȝecpanȝ.
Ealpa æpert.
Eoþðbuenðpa
Liuðlaþer runu.
Ẏmbe hẏne ȝoðpa fæla.
Dpeaþflacpa hpæþ.
Dpæfen panðpoðe.
Speant anð realo bpun.
† Spupð-leoma rtoð.
Spẏlce eal Finnrbupuh.
Fẏnenu pæþe.
Ne ȝefpæȝn ic.
Næfne puþþlicoþ.
Æt peþa hilðe.
Sixtiȝ riȝebeoþna.
Sel ȝebæpann.
Ne nefpne rpa noc hpitne meðo.
Sel fonȝẏlban.
Donne hnæfe ȝulban.
Dir hæȝrtealbar.
Diȝ fuhton fif ðaȝar.
Spa hẏpa nan ne feol.
Dpihtȝeriða.

Ac hiȝ ða ðupu heolðon.
Da ȝepat him punð hæleð.
On pæȝ ȝanȝan.
Sæðe þ̄ hir bẏnne.

Abpocen pæþe.
Deþe rceoppum hþoþ.
Anð eac pæþ hir helm ðẏpl.
Da hine rona fpæȝn.

Folcer hẏþðe.
Du ða piȝenð hẏpa.
Funða ȝenæron.
Oð�ðe hpæþeþ ðæþa hẏṛra.

FINNSBURH

Fragment and Episode

Edited by Donald K. Fry

Methuen & Co Ltd
11 NEW FETTER LANE
LONDON EC4P 4EE

First published in 1974 by Methuen & Co Ltd
Copyright © 1974 Introduction, Notes etc.
Donald K. Fry
Printed in Great Britain by
Butler & Tanner Ltd, Frome and London

SBN 416 78930 7

Distributed in the USA by
HARPER & ROW PUBLISHERS INC.
BARNES & NOBLE IMPORT DIVISION

CONTENTS

For Arthur Hutson

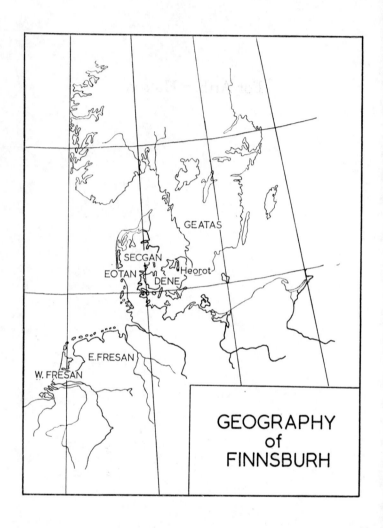

GEOGRAPHY
of
FINNSBURH

PREFACE

This edition of the Finnsburh Episode and Fragment incorpor-
ates several innovations which I hope will find favour and
further use among Anglo-Saxon scholars. First, all textual
variants are fully glossed. Variants prove useless to the reader
unless he can translate them, and even the most experienced
scholar might have difficulty with entries such as Trautmann's
coinage *swinsað. Second, glossary entries record the word's
meanings in the language as a whole, not just in the immediate
context, so that readers can see the possible range of denota-
tions and connotations, appreciate word play and puns, and
escape some of the danger of contextual glossing becoming a
form of covert editorial interpretation. Third, glossary entries
record literal meanings in so far as possible, especially in com-
pounds. (One editor glossed *Elene* 651a *dareð-lacende* as 'war-
rior', thus dropping two vivid images, the spear and its
'player', from the reader's consciousness.) To facilitate diction
studies, the glossary cross-references second elements of com-
pounds, and notes which elements occur only in poetry.

The textual editing turns on conservative principles.
Hickes's transcript has an undeservedly poor reputation as a
record of viable readings in its lost manuscript, opening the
floodgates of emendation, not only on itself but by kindred
impulse on the Episode as well; for example, Trautmann's
1904 edition introduces 44 changes in the 48 lines of the
Fragment. My version lets the *Beowulf* manuscript and Hickes's
text stand so long as each reading meets two tests: (1) each
half-line must contain two strong stresses, at least four syllables,
and proper alliteration; and (2) each word must make gram-
matical and semantic sense in context. I admit 16 emenda-
tions in 145 lines. In so far as possible, I have tried to draw
my interpretation from the edited text, rather than vice versa.

I wish to acknowledge the assistance so many people have
given me on this project. The staffs of the British Museum,

the Lambeth Palace Library (especially E. G. W. Bill), the Alderman Library of the University of Virginia, the Melville Library at Stony Brook, and the University College London Library extended privileges and services graciously. The University of Virginia provided two large grants and several smaller ones to finance travel and xeroxing. Numerous students and colleagues helped along the way, especially Fred Heinemann, Phyllis Leffingwell, David Thelen, Carol Wolf, and Hoyt Duggan. I must thank especially Martin Stevens and Alan Bliss for saving me from several philological disasters; uncaught errors, of course, are mine, and I would appreciate notice of any and all mistakes. *English Language Notes* kindly permitted me to incorporate material from my notes in their volumes 6 and 8.

I wish to thank my editors, Arthur Brown, Alan Bliss, and Patrick Taylor, for their patience with a long-overdue typescript, and my wife Joan, who dutifully sent me back to the study in fine weather.

Stony Brook, New York   DONALD K. FRY
October 1972

ABBREVIATIONS

Bracketed numbers refer to bibliography entries.

AfdA	*Anzeiger für deutsches Altertum*
And	*Andreas*
ANF	*Arkiv för Nordisk Filologi*
Archiv	*Archiv für das Studium der Neueren Sprachen und Literaturen*
ASC	*Anglo-Saxon Chronicle*, ed. C. Plummer (Oxford, 1892–1899), cited by Ms and date
Ayr	Ayres [48]
Bede	Bede's *Historiam Ecclesiasticam Gentis Anglorum*, ed. C. Plummer (Oxford, 1896)
Beiträge	*Beiträge zur Geschichte der deutschen Sprache und Literatur*
Bgg	Bugge [273]
Blt	Bolton revision of Wrenn [2244]
Brb	*Battle of Brunanburh*
Brd	Brodeur [230]
BT	*Anglo-Saxon Dictionary*, ed. J. Bosworth (Oxford, 1898)
BTS	Supplement to BT, ed. T. N. Toller (Oxford, 1921)
Bwf	*Beowulf*
Chb	Chambers [307]
Chr	*Christ*
Cmb	*Old English Grammar*, ed. A. Campbell (Oxford, 1959), cited by paragraphs
Cnb	Conybeare [355]
Dan	*Daniel*
DbB	Dobbie [480]
DbM	Dobbie [481]
Dkn	Dickens [475]
EETS	Early English Text Society
Ele	*Elene*
ELN	*English Language Notes*
ESt	*Englische Studien*
Etm	Etmüller [550]
Exo	*Exodus*
Fep	Finnsburh Episode (*Beowulf* 1063–1160a)
Fnb	*Finnsburh Fragment*
Gen	*Genesis*

xiii

GfM	*Gifts of Men*
Glc	*Guthlac*
Grn 1	Grein [675]
Grn 2	Grein [676]
Grv	Girvan [637]
GtB	Grundtvig [704]
GtD	Grundtvig [707]
HbM	*Husband's Message*
Hks	Hickes [818]
Hlt	Holthausen [845], cited by editions
HMD	*Concise Anglo-Saxon Dictionary*, ed. J. R. C. Hall and H. D. Meritt (Cambridge, 1960)
Hyn	Heyne [815]
JEGP	*Journal of English and Germanic Philology*
Jul	*Juliana*
Klb	Klaeber [1026], 3rd ed. with 2 supplements unless otherwise noted
Klg	Kluge [1080]
Klp	Klipstein [1078]
Kmb	Kemble [989], cited by editions
LwB	Lawrence [1188]
LwF	Lawrence [1190]
Mak	Mackie [1289]
Mal	Malone [1326]
Mld	*Battle of Maldon*
MLN	*Modern Language Notes*
Mlr	Möller [1460]
MLR	*Modern Language Review*
MlW	Malone [1393]
Ms	Manuscript
NED	*Oxford English Dictionary* (Oxford, 1933)
NM	*Neuphilologische Mitteilungen*
Phx	*Phoenix*
PMLA	*Publications of the Modern Language Association*
PPs	*Paris Psalter*
Rdl	*Riddle*
Rgr	Rieger [1705]
Sdg	Sedgefield [1892], cited by editions
SdV	Sedgefield [1891]
Sfr	*Seafarer*
Shk	Schücking [1851]
Shl	Schaldemose [1787]

Soc	Heyne [815], 5th ed. by A. Socin
Sprachschatz	*Sprachschatz der angelsächsischen Dichter*, ed. C. W. M. Grein, F. Holthausen, and J. J. Köhler (Heidelberg 1912–1914)
Thp	Thorpe [2084]
TrB	Trautmann [2106]
TrF	Trautmann [2109]
WCh	Wyatt [2267], revised by R. W. Chambers
Wds	*Widsith*
Whl	*Whale*
Wld	*Waldere*
Wlk 1	Wülker [2264]
Wlk 2	Wülker [2259]
Wms	Williams [2221]
Wnd	*Wanderer*
Wrn	Wrenn [2244]
ZDA	*Zeitschrift für deutsches Altertum und deutsche Literatur*
ZDP	*Zeitschrift für deutsche Philologie*

Introduction

I THE MANUSCRIPTS

The text of the *Finnsburh Fragment* derives from a lost manu-
script transcribed by George Hickes before 1705, and the
Finnsburh Episode comprises lines 1063–1160a of *Beowulf*. Hickes
printed the text of the Fragment in his *Linguarum Vett. Septen-
trionalium Thesaurus* (Oxford, 1705), volume I, pages 192–193,
partially reproduced here as the frontispiece, under the follow-
ing caption: 'Eodem metro conditum forte reperi fragmenti
poëtici singulare folium, in codice MS. homiliarum *Semi-
Saxonicarum* qui extat in Bibliotheca *Lambethana*.' Only two
codices now in the Lambeth Palace Library fit this descrip-
tion.[1] Manuscript 487 is a thirteenth-century collection of
Anglo-Saxon homilies and probably the codex in question.
Written on vellum sheets 7 by 5·25 inches, it contains 67 folios
with 28 lines to a page. Hickes, in a note on page 222, calls it
'cod. Ms. homil. *Semi-Sax*'. Manuscript 489 contains eight
homilies, five by Ælfric, probably copied in the eleventh cen-
tury, but the language is not what Hickes normally called
'semi-Saxon'. Ms 489 has 58 vellum folios, 7·5 by 4·75 inches,
with 19 lines to the page until folio 21b, then 25 lines per
page. Neither codex now contains the Fragment, nor have
repeated searches of the Lambeth Palace Library by numerous
editors, myself included, turned it up. Hickes's description
indicates only that a codex contained it, but not necessarily
bound in; it may have formed part of an earlier binding or
merely a loose leaf. Edmund Gibson's catalogue of the
library, compiled early in the eighteenth century, does
not mention it; but then few catalogues before Humphrey

---

[1] M. R. James and C. Jenkins, *A Descriptive Catalogue of the Manuscripts
in the Library of Lambeth Palace* (Cambridge: Cambridge Univ. Press, 1930),
673–91.

Wanley's were exhaustive.[2] Wanley himself sets it apart by ruled lines from the rest of the Lambeth entries and describes it as follows: 'Fragmentum Poeticum, praelium quoddam describens in oppido Finnisburgh nuncupato innitum, quod exhibuit D. Hickesius. Gramm. Anglo-Sax. p. 192.'[3] The unusual ruled lines and the lack of any manuscript description seem to indicate that Wanley never actually saw the Fragment, so it was probably lost after its transcription sometime before 1703, when volume I of the *Thesaurus* was in proof, and perhaps as early as 1699. In the absence of evidence to the contrary, we may assume that Hickes transcribed the text himself. Scholars have generally regarded him as a careless copyist,[4] an opinion which has resulted in extensive and largely unwarranted emendation of the text. He commonly errs in confusing *u* for *a* (3a, 25b, and perhaps 42b), and in Ð for þ. Ritchie Girvan, noting that Hickes and Wanley, the latter a most careful copyist, make similar errors, imputes the inaccuracies to their printer.[5] Hickes used no punctuation in his text except a period after every half-line; he capitalized the first word in each verse, all proper names, and four other words: *Eastan* 3a, *Nama* 24a, *Celæs* 29a, and *Finnsburuh* 36a. The division between pages 192 and 193 in the *Thesaurus* comes between *driht-gesiða* and *ac* in line 42.

The Finnsburh Episode occupies folios 156a–158b (153a–155b in the 'old foliation') of British Museum Manuscript Cotton Vitellius A. XV, the '*Beowulf* Codex', actually two unrelated codices, the first containing King Alfred's translation of St Augustine's *Soliloquies*, *The Gospel of Nicodemus*, *Solomon and Saturn*, and a fragment of a *Passio Quintini*. To this collection a seventeenth-century binder added a fragmentary life of St Christopher, *The Wonders of the East*, *Alexander's Letter to Aristotle*, *Beowulf*, and the *Judith* fragment, all tales of wonders,

---

[2] Ker [1000] item 282, p. 344. Gibson's catalogue is an undated manuscript book, Lambeth Palace Library Records, F. 39; my thanks to E. G. W. Bill for this reference.

[3] Volume II of Hickes, 269, published in 1705.

[4] *E.g.*, Chb 245. n. 1.

[5] Grv 329.

especially giants. Nothing is known of the early provenance of the manuscript until it appeared in the collection of the famous antiquarian Sir Robert Bruce Cotton (1571–1631), except that Lawrence Nowell, Dean of Lichfield and an early Old English scholar, signed the first page, dating his signature 1563. The Cotton collection passed to the Crown after various seventeenth-century vicissitudes, and was housed eventually in Ashburnham House, which occupied the site of the present House of Lords. In 1731 fire destroyed about 200 of the 958 manuscript volumes and damaged many others, including Vitellius A. XV. The heat rendered the outside edges of the pages brittle, and they progressively crumbled until preservative steps were taken in the nineteenth century. Luckily the Icelander G. J. Thorkelin and a scribe made two transcripts in 1787, now housed in the Royal Library at Copenhagen, which preserved many readings since lost in the manuscript.[6]

Beowulf is written in two scribal hands, shifting at line 1939; both date from about the year 1000, give or take two decades, corresponding with the dates of the other three major Old English poetic codices.[7] Neither the handwriting nor the illustrations of other works in the codex give any reliable indications for localizing the scriptorium. The text is written on vellum, and folios 156a–158b contain twenty lines of script per page spaced as prose.

The punctuation is rather haphazard. Lines 1063–1160a contain only three capitals (*Gewiton* 1125a, *Swa* 1142a, and perhaps *Syþðan* 1077b), five accents, all on long vowels (*bán-fatu*, *dón* 1116, *blód* 1121b, *hám* 1147b, and *sǽ-siðe* 1149a), and 18 periods (after *wrecen* 1065b, *þorfte* 1071b, *com* 1077b, *meðel-stede* 1082b, *gefeohtan* 1083b, *ðegne* 1085a, *wolde* 1094b, *benemde* 1097b, *bræce* 1100b, *inge-gold* 1107b, *eal-gylden* 1111b, *crungon* 1113b, *astah* 1118b, *multon* 1120b, *ætspranc* 1121b, *scacen* 1124b, *gemunde* 1141b. and *læddon* 1159a), all but the last marking the end of a half-line. The folio divisions follow: folio 156a *þær* 1063a–*gare* 1075a; 156b *wunde* 1075a–*aðum* 1097b; 157a

[6] K. Malone, *The Thorkelin Transcripts of Beowulf*, Early English Manuscripts in Facsimile, I (Copenhagen, 1951; London, 1952).
[7] Ker [1000] item 216.

benemde 1097b–*Wand* 1119a; 157b *to* 1119a–*swiðor* 1139a;
158a *þohte* 1139a–*læddon* 1159a; 158b *to* 1159a–end.

II LANGUAGE AND DATE [8]

Despite the possibility of errors introduced by Hickes as trans-
criber and by his printer, both the Finnsburh Fragment and
Episode appear to be written in the late West Saxon dialect,
with some admixture of Anglian, Northumbrian, and Kentish
forms resulting either from successive stages of copying or
from the normal presence of these forms in West Saxon poetic
diction. Typical late West Saxon forms are *scypon* 1154b,
hwylc 1104a, and *scyneð* 7b (showing late West Saxon *y* for
early West Saxon *i*), *buruhþelu* 30b and *Finnsburuh* 36b (intru-
sive -*u*-). *Willað* 9b is an early West Saxon form, but compare
wylle 27b, which is late; *Beowulf* contains this mixture as well
in 23 occurrences.

Several Anglian forms appear. *Wæg* 43b shows Anglian *æ*
for West Saxon *e*, but the form is found occasionally in other
dialects; for *mænig* 13a, see Cmb 193d, n. 4. *Mehte* 1082a
shows *e* for West Saxon broken *ea* before *h* and a consonant, a
characteristic shared by Anglian, Kentish, and late West
Saxon texts; but Alfred's *Orosius* frequently has *mehte* (Cmb
312). *Eþ-gesyne* 1110b has *ē* for early West Saxon *īe*, *i*-umlaut
of *ēa*, characteristic of Anglian and Kentish. Klb xcv lists
nemne 1081b and *morðor-* 1079a, 1105a as Anglian vocabulary
for West Saxon *butan* and *morð*.

Northumbrian forms are present too. *Hwearflicra* 34a has
ea for *eo*, perhaps northern Northumbrian. *Sword* 15b and
worold- 1080a and 1142b show late Northumbrian *wo* for *weo*,
but these forms may be West Saxon; see also *worcum* 1100a.
Heordra 26a may have Northumbrian confusion of *ea* and *eo*,
but West Saxon parallels are not lacking.

Some Kentish forms occur. *Cweþ* 24a has *e* for West Saxon
æ, possibly late Kentish or Mercian, but the phrase '*cweþ he*'
is suspicious (see line note). The first element of *meþelstede*
1082b belongs to this class. *Nefre* 39a is Kentish, but compare

[8] This discussion is based primarily on Klb lxxi–cxxiv.

næfre 1b, 37a. *Scefte* 7a has *e* for West Saxon *ea* after initial palatal *sc*, Kentish and occasionally Mercian, but also late West Saxon.

None of these forms conclusively proves non-West Saxon composition, nor do they help date the poems. However, if we accept *Beowulf* 1382a *wundini* as an archaic instrumental form, then the poem was written down no later than A.D. 750 (see Wrn 34–5). Although dates ranging from 650 to 1000 have been proposed, scholars generally accept 725 as the probable date of *Beowulf*'s composition, with the Fragment roughly contemporary. Northumbria is generally thought to be the place of origin because of the high state of culture there in the eighth century, although East Anglia has gained recently as a candidate because of the possible connections with the Sutton Hoo shipburial.[9]

III THE STORY

The greatest difficulty in Finnsburh scholarship is establishing the plot. The *Beowulf* poet typically tells his digressions in allusive style, evoking by a few details stories he could assume his audience knew from the ambience of traditional legends in a culture whose primary entertainment was narrative song. The Episode tells us very little in general about the events at Finn's *burh*, concentrating its detailed segments on the truce terms, the funeral, and Hengest's later thoughts. The Fragment, on the other hand, spells out its story in great detail and resultant verisimilitude, but covers only about a fifth of the action. In addition, scholars have complicated the critical issues involved by some rather shaky extra-textual assumptions, *e.g.*, that the Anglo-Saxons could not sail in winter, often resulting in unnecessary emendations. Furthermore, the 145 lines of the combined texts contain 40 *hapax legomena*, averaging one for every seven verses; seven of these *hapax legomena* have extremely problematical meanings. Even some of the better attested words, such as *eoten-*, *styrode*, and *swanas*

---

[9] See, *e.g.*, R. L. S. Bruce-Mitford, 'Sutton Hoo and the Background to the Poem', supplement to Girvan [636], 2nd ed., esp. pp. 96–8.

add trouble by unusual meanings, and the syntax occasionally proves tricky, *e.g.*, 5, 1106. All of these factors make interpretation difficult. Here I shall review the more prominent attempts at delineating the plot, and offer a new version of my own.

Most interpretations of the Finnsburh story belong to one of two camps, depending on whether the attack described in the Fragment is assigned to the events preceding or following the truce between Hengest and Finn. Hermann Möller's theory assumes the latter, as shown in this summary:

> Finn, king of the Frisians, had carried off Hildeburh, daughter of Hoc . . . , probably with her consent. Her father Hoc seems to have pursued the fugitives, and to have been slain in the fight which ensued on his overtaking them. After the lapse of some twenty years, the brothers Hnæf and Hengest, Hoc's sons, were old enough to undertake the duty of avenging their father's death. They make an inroad into Finn's country. A battle takes place in which many warriors, among them Hnæf and a son of Finn . . ., are killed. Peace is therefore solemnly concluded, and the slain warriors are burnt. . . . As the year is too far advanced for Hengest to return home . . . , he and those of his men who survive remain for the winter in the Frisian country with Finn. But Hengest's thoughts dwell constantly on the death of his brother Hnæf, and he would gladly welcome any excuse to break the peace which has been sworn by both parties. His ill-concealed desire for revenge is noticed by the Frisians, who anticipate it by themselves taking the initiative and attacking Hengest and his men whilst they are sleeping in the hall. *This is the night attack described in the Fragment.* It would seem that after a brave and desperate resistance Hengest himself falls in this fight, but two of his retainers, Guthlaf and Oslaf, succeed in cutting their way through their enemies and in escaping to their own land. They return with fresh troops, attack and slay Finn, and carry his queen Hildeburh off with them.[10]

[10] Mlr, summary by Chb 254–5.

As Chambers observes, Möller's interpretation has no textual support whatever, depending largely on parallels with the stories of Hild and Gudrun. Furthermore, the Fragment mentions Hnæf as alive, whereas in the Episode Hnæf's body rests on the pyre (*æt Hnæfes ade* 1114b) before the winter preceding the second fight. The *hearo-geong cyning* of 2b should be Hnæf, since he and Finn are the only kings present, and Finn is old enough to have a fighting son, which makes him unlikely to be *hearo-geong*. So the Fragment battle most likely results from the initial attack.

The other school of interpretation, clustering around Sophus Bugge's analysis, begins with the assumption that the Fragment describes the first attack. Most scholars today accept this view, despite radical divergences over details. In 1915, W. W. Lawrence summarized the Bugge view:

Finn, king of the Frisians, has married a Danish princess, Hildeburg, the daughter of Hoc. Hildeburg's brother Hnæf, accompanied by a band of Danish warriors, is staying at Finnsburg, the residence of Finn in Friesland. The Danes are quartered by themselves in a hall. For reasons with which we are not acquainted – probably an old feud between Frisians and Danes, temporarily healed by the marriage of Hildeburg – Finn attacks his visitors as they are sleeping in the hall at night. The Danes make a brave and successful defence. This defence is described in the *Finnsburg Fragment.* . . . Hnæf, probably with a companion, has been on the watch. There are sixty men inside the hall, of whom Hengest, Sigeferth, Eaha, Ordlaf, and Guthlaf are particularly mentioned. The attacking party is discovered by the gleam of moonlight on their weapons or armor. Hnæf arouses his men, who immediately rush to the doors to prevent the enemy from entering. Garulf, an impetuous warrior of the Frisian party, is restrained by Guthere from at once attacking, but Garulf demands the name of the warrior defending the door, and receives from Sigeferth a defiant reply. Restraining himself no longer, Garulf, followed by the rest, rushes to the attack, and is the first to fall. For five days the struggle continues, but not a single Dane is killed. Then a chief of the attacking party withdraws. . . . According to the *Episode*, Hnæf is killed, and the fight takes place in a single night. Hengest, a thane of Hnæf, assumes the leadership upon the death of his lord. All of Finn's thanes save a few have been slain, so that he can no longer continue the combat. The Frisians therefore offer terms of peace, agreeing, on their part, to give the Danes a hall of their own, to allow them equal power with the Frisians, and an equal share of treasure, when this is dispensed by Finn to his warriors. It is further agreed that the Frisians are to treat the Danes with great courtesy, not recalling the feud, nor taunting them with following the leader of the men who slew their lord. The Danish part of the bargain seems to consist solely in giving allegiance to Finn. These promises are duly confirmed by oath. A great funeral pyre is erected, upon which the dead warriors, chief among them Hnæf and a son of Queen Hildeburg, are burnt. Frisians and Danes then settle down for the winter. At the coming of spring, when travel by sea becomes possible, Hengest, who has been nursing his desire for revenge, sails away. The subsequent events are exceedingly obscure. Apparently Hengest reaches Denmark and brings back reinforcements, and perhaps he is presented by 'the son of Hunlaf', probably a Dane, with a supremely good sword. It is clear, however, that Finn is slain in his own home, after bitter reproaches have been uttered by Guthlaf and Oslaf. The Danes then plunder Finn's treasures, and sail back to Denmark with this booty and with Queen Hildeburg.[11]

The main points are: the Fragment's attack precipitates all subsequent events; Finn offers terms to Hengest, who has succeeded the dead Hnæf; Hengest accepts; the Danes live with Finn all winter; and the Danes eventually avenge Hnæf.

Most of the subsequent interpretation has dealt with Hen-

[11] Bgg, summarized by LwF 428–9.

gest's revenge. In 1917, Henry Morgan Ayres tried to meta-morphose Hengest into a romantic hero:

> Hengest is in an acutely tragic situation; he is personally responsible for putting his followers and himself in the position of living on with the man who had murdered their lord. The conflict of duty is a nice one; torn between his oath to Finn and his duty to the dead Hnæf, with trouble likely to break out among his men at any moment, what are Hengest's emotions, what is he going to do? Here is a complication which demands unravelling. It is a perfect balance, of the sort dear to the temperament and traditions that gave birth to Hamlet. Is there not also, in some sense, a tragedy of Hengest?[12]

Hengest–Hamlet suffers with his problems: 'Occasions gross as earth informed against him. While he was debating with himself . . . his followers began an egging. . . . What happens first is that the son of Hunlaf . . . offers him a sword. . . . This act of Hunlafing had one very clear object, to summon Hengest to vengeance' (Ayr 292). Further, 'Hengest's almost blunted purpose was not whetted by Hunlafing alone. The latter's uncles, Guðlaf and Oslaf, . . . took occasion to mention to Hengest the fierce attack (the one, presumably, in which Hnæf had fallen); cast up to him all the troubles that had befallen them ever since their disastrous sea-journey to Finnsburg. . . . The effect of all this on Hengest is cumulative. Where he was before in perfect balance, he is now wrought to actions by the words of his followers; he can control himself no longer; the balance is destroyed. . . . Vengeance wins the day.'[13]

In 1926, Kemp Malone offered a new reconstruction of the later events in the Episode, while generally agreeing with Bugge and Lawrence's version of the story as a whole. Beginning with line 1138, he translates: 'he thought not so much of the voyage as of revenge: whether he might bring on a battle, in which he would be mindful of the children of the

[12] Ayr 290.
[13] Ayr 293–4; the interpretation in Wms is rather far-fetched, but useful in details.

Euts, since [*swa*] he did not prevent [*forwyrnde*] his lord [*woroldrædende* < Ms *woroldrædenne*] when he [Hnæf] laid in his [Hengest's] lap Hunlafing, the battlegleamer, the best of bills; its edges were known to the Euts'.[14] Malone draws a scenario accounting for the sword: 'the dying Hnæf with all solemnity gives his own sword to Hengest, the famous sword Hunlafing, which in the battle then still raging against the Frisians had done good service. Hnæf lays his sword in Hengest's lap, and Hengest does not prevent him from so doing, *i.e.*, Hengest accepts the gift and with it accepts the task of avenging the death of its former owner' (Mal 167). Malone reconstructs the sequence of events in the actual vengeance as follows: 'the escape of Guthlaf and Oslaf and their voyage home to Denmark; . . . their report to their fellow-Danes; . . . the agitation among the Danes; . . . the voyage to Frisia of a Danish fleet, and its attack on Finn at his hall' (Mal 169).

In 1943, A. G. Brodeur attacked Malone's translation of 1142–4 by demonstrating convincingly that there is 'no evidence anywhere that the *-ing* suffix was ever used to form sword names from the names of their current or former owners'.[15] Against Malone's contention that the *Beowulf* poet 'never uses a patronymic except in connection with the true name',[16] and that 'Hunlafing' therefore must be not the name of a person but of a sword, Brodeur concludes from Germanic examples that 'the true name does *not* require to be expressed, so long as the patronymic suffices, alone or in combination with other epithets, to identify the person designated' (Brd 350). Brodeur then concludes:

> *Hūnlāfing* is best interpreted as 'son of Hunlaf'. But once this is established, it overthrows Malone's interpretation of the whole passage. For if it was Hunlafing who gave Hengest the sword, then *woroldrǽdenne* cannot refer to Hnæf: it would be absurd to say that 'Hengest did not prevent Hnæf when the son of Hunlaf placed a sword on

14 Mal 158–9, translating 1138b–45.
15 Brd 332–3.   16 Malone [1341] 302–3.

his lap'. Hnæf was dead when Hunlafing gave Hengest the sword. Therefore there is no necessity for taking *worold-rædenne* as a title: it is better to keep the MS reading and regard the word as the abstract noun *woroldræden(n)*, thing object of *ne forwyrnde*. Therefore *swā* cannot mean 'since'; for the clause which it introduces can no longer be regarded as looking backward to the effect of an action by Hnæf; rather it looks forward to the performance of an action by the son of Hunlaf. Thus lines 1142–1145 should be taken . . .: Hengest, already eager to avenge Hnæf's death, did not refuse the course of action universally approved when Hunlaf's son laid on his lap a sword. It was this act, and Hengest's reaction to it – his acceptance of the sword, and with it his acceptance of the obligation to avenge – which resolved Hengest's tragic dilemma (Brd 354–5).

In 1953, E. V. K. Dobbie distilled previous scholarship into the following reconstruction:

Hnæf, a prince of the Scyldings, is the brother of Hildeburh, the queen of King Finn of the Frisians. . . . During a visit made to Finn's court by Hnæf and a body of his retainers . . ., a fight broke out between Danes and Frisians, in which Hnæf was killed. This fight is the one described in the Fragment. The immediate cause of the hostilities is not clear, but in ll. 1071–72a a hint is given that the *Eotan* (usually identified as Jutes) bore a heavy responsibility for the trouble. The result of the fighting was a stalemate; Hnæf's men, leaderless in a foreign country and without resources, were in the utmost peril, while Finn's forces had been so depleted that he was unable to bring about a decisive victory. Finn therefore concluded a truce with Hengest, now leader of the surviving Danes. . . . This truce was clearly nothing more than a temporary expedient, intended to serve until the winter was over and the Danes could return home. . . . The truce lasted, apparently without incident, through the remainder of the winter; but with the coming of spring Hengest's mind, until then preoccupied with the desire to return to his own land, turned to the possibility of revenge for his lord's death and for the injuries . . . which had been done to the Danes. Receiving a clear reminder of his duty in the form of a sword presented by one of his followers, and goaded by the reproaches of Guthlaf and Oslaf, Hengest attacked Finn in his own hall, in spite of the truce to which he had consented, and killed him amid his warriors. The Danes carried away the Frisian queen to her own people, together with Finn's royal treasure.[17]

Most scholars today accept this version of the plot.

My own reconstruction essentially follows Dobbie's summary, with three modifications concerning the role of the *eoten-*, Hengest's motives, and the confused events in lines 1138b–51a. The context of the Episode in *Beowulf* also becomes important, for we must keep in mind the surrounding analogous circumstances and the point of view from which the poet tells the story. Hrothgar's *scop* provides the entertainment at the banquet celebrating Beowulf's victory over Grendel. This feud has lasted for twelve dreary years, during which no Dane could manage to kill Grendel as he continued ambushing and ejecting them from their hall every night. This Heorot-hall stands as the symbol of Hrothgar's empire ('its light shone over many lands', 311). Furthermore, it symbolizes civilization amid political chaos and hostile nature. Equally important emblems of civilization and of *this* civilization are the joys of drinking and treasure-giving in the hall. Yet this very joy enrages the monster lurking in the figurative and literal darkness under the land, and brings him forth to destroy it. Hrothgar cannot come to terms with Grendel except by sharing Heorot with the monster: the king holds court with his retainers by day, and Grendel rules alone at night. Hrothgar waits, his only option, until the qualified hero arrives.

The hall has suffered from the wrestling of Beowulf and Grendel. Only the roof is intact, and we can imagine the benches slightly askew on their cracked supports, the door splintered from Grendel's touch. And though Grendel to all

[17] DbB xlvii–xlviii.

appearances seems dead, no one has seen the corpse, and monsters have a habit of reappearing at the worse moment.

In this hall and in this uneasy circumstance, the *scop* sings of Finnsburh, and his very song forms part of the restoration of order symbolized by hall-joy. But he must be tactful. Grendel's twelve years have shamed the Danes, and a foreigner has accomplished what they could not. So the *scop* evokes in his song their glorious past by reciting a famous Danish victory achieved against formidable odds and agonizing circumstances.[18]

One analogue precedes the Episode, and a second follows it. The poet has just reminded us in lines 1017–19 of the underlying treachery of the Hrothulf intrigue, which will result in a *coup d'état* upon Hrothgar's death; and against this undercurrent, the poet will set Wealhtheow's desperate but futile peacemaking in lines 1216–31. As early as lines 82b–85, the poet calls attention to the impending hall-combat in the Heathobard feud, which will erupt despite the best efforts of Hrothgar's daughter Freawaru. This princess and her mother share the role of *freoðuwebbe* 'peace-weaver'; of Hildeburh's situation we know nothing except that she is a foreign princess. Neither the Fragment nor the Episode mentions a feud preceding Hnæf's visit, but perhaps Hildeburh has been married to Finn in an effort to patch up old frictions between the Frisians and the Danes or Hocings.[19] Even if she has not, the three queens share the experience of sudden destruction of their relatively stable situations by violence.[20]

The Episode opens with Hildeburh's discovery of hall-combat in progress, and the *scop* comments, 'Ne huru Hildeburh herian þorfte/*eotena treowe*' (1071–72a), usually translated 'Nor indeed did Hildeburh need to praise the trustworthiness of the *eotena*'. No sentence in Finnsburh scholarship

---

[18] See LwF 387–9 and 429, and Wms 11. For the opposite view, see Brodeur [231] 40–1. [19] See Bonjour [159] 44–63.

[20] Hygelac's queen Hygd undergoes similar disasters later in the poem, as does the old woman who presides at Beowulf's funeral. Grendel's mother, despite her monster role, also fits the pattern. Brodeur [231] 35 notices that a woman is also involved in Cynewulf and Cyneheard's feud, *ASC* A755.

has caused more trouble than this one. Most editors have capitalized *eotena*, translating the word as the name of the Jutes, a northern European Germanic tribe eventually involved in the Saxon conquest of Britain. But the Anglian forms should be genitive plural *Eot(e)na*, dative plural *Eotum* (or, by analogy, *Eotenum*, *Eotonum*), corresponding to late West Saxon *Ytena* and *Ytum*; Chambers explains the inconsistency as scribal error.[21] If the *Eotena* are Jutes, then their treacherous role requires an explanation of their presence in Frisia and their assignment to one side or the other. Chambers cautions, 'All that we are justified in deducing from the text is that Frisians and *Eotenas* are both under the command of Finn', but goes on to suggest that the Jutes are subject to Finn, or mercenaries in his service. Chambers insists that Finn remained blameless in the attack on the Danes, and so finds the Jutes, whatever their capacity, convenient villains (Chb 268–89). Sedgefield equates Jutes and Frisians, suggesting that 'the poet, living at the end of the seventh or the beginning of the eighth century, may have regarded the names "Frisians" and "Jutes" as synonyms for Finn's subjects'.[22] Girvan regarded these Jutes as Hengest's troops, subordinate to Hnæf, citing 1141 *þæt he eotena bearn inne gemunde*, translated, 'so that he should remember the sons of the Jutes' [*sic*] in the sense of avenge them . . . an absurdity if the Jutes were the enemy.[23] Dobbie cautiously regards the Eoten as 'Jutish allies or dependents of Finn who were staying at Finnsburh at the time of Hnæf's visit'.[24] Wrenn complicates the issue unnecessarily with his suggestion that 'there may have been two Jutish groups—the one in Danish service called Healfdene at l. 1069 and Dene at l. 1090, and the other under Finn who ruled the Frisians'.[25]

Whoever the *eoten-* are, they are probably not Danes and not subject to Hengest. The references in lines 1141, *þæt he eotena bearn inne gemunde* and 1145, *þæs wæron mid eotenum ecge*

[21] Chb 261, and see Klb 233, n. 3.

[22] Sedgefield [1894] 481.   [23] Grv 352–3.

[24] DbB xlix; Brodeur [231] 33 ff. concurs.

[25] Wrenn, revision of Chb 544. Alan Bliss tells me that Tolkien first suggested this idea in unpublished lectures.

cuðe, are ambiguous. Hengest may be recalling dead friends or live enemies in the first, and the sword's edges may be direly remembered among the enemies or famous among the Danes in the latter. But in 1087b–88a, *þæt hie healfre geweald/wið eotena bearn agan moston*, the context seems to require that the *eoten-* be neither Danes, nor in Danish service, since the truce terms require equal sharing and justice for Hengest's and Finn's retainers. So the *eoten-*, whether Jutes or not, would seem to be among (if not the same as) Finn's troops.

Recently R. E. Kaske has suggested that 'the Jutes (*Eotan*) are never mentioned in *Beowulf*; that in all the passages quoted above the words in question are in fact declensional forms of *eoten* and should be rendered . . . "giants"; and that throughout the Finn episode . . . the term is to be understood as a hostile epithet for the Frisians'.[26] Besides regarding *eoten-* as an 'insulting figurative epithet for "enemies" ', Kaske offers evidence for 'giants' as a Scandinavian term of insult and for identification of the Frisians and Finn as giants in early Germanic culture. Furthermore, he finds some evidence for traditional hostility between Danes and Frisians (Kaske, 289 ff. and n. 12).

Juxtaposing these possibilities against the context in *Beowulf* sketched above, we have the *scop* reciting a tale of Danish victory against their traditional enemies, the Frisians, and availing himself of an epithet of scorn which provides an alternative alliteration to *Fres-* and *Finn*. In 1071–72a, the term proves especially appropriate where Hildeburh apparently reviews the cause of the battle she awakens to find in progress. This ascription of blame to the Frisians accords well with the beginning of the Fragment, where the Danes are clearly being attacked from the outside by Finn's troops. But there is another possibility. Hildeburh awakens to find a battle going on, yet the sentences on either side of 1071–72a, likewise in the past tense, refer to events probably in the

---

[26] R. E. Kaske, 'The *Eotenas* in *Beowulf*', in *Old English Poetry, Fifteen Essays*, ed. R. P. Creed (Providence: Brown Univ. Press, 1967), 286, ultimately based on Rieger [1708]; Kaske disagrees with Rieger's identification of *eoten-* in lines 1072 and 1145 as Danes.

future, the death of Hnæf and her son. The phrase *eotena treowe* may refer not to the perpetrators of the first attack, but to the later truce. *Treow* means 'treaty, agreement' as well as 'trust, trustworthiness', as in *Exodus* 422–6:

> þæt þu wið waldend   wære heolde,
> fæste treowe,   seo þe freoðo sceal
> in lifdagum,   lengest weorðan,
> awa to aldre   unswiciendo.
> Hu þearf mannes sunu   maran treowe?

(that you have kept the treaty with the Ruler, a steadfast agreement, which shall be unwavering peace for as long as your life-days, forever and ever. Does the son of man need a greater agreement?)[27] Lines 1071–72a may refer ahead to Finn and Hengest's treaty, which the queen had no need to praise, simply because it failed to ensure peace, again under-lining the parallel situations of Hildeburh and the other tragic queens in *Beowulf*. The sentence may also refer to both incidents, the attack and the treaty.

Now I shall discuss the continuing controversy over Hen-gest's motives, which begins with Ayres's 1917 article, labelling the Finnsburh story as 'a tragedy of Hengest, hesitating, like Shakespeare's Hamlet, over the duty of revenge' (Chb 266). The key word here is 'hesitating', and to understand Hen-gest's possible motives for doing so, we must examine the mores involved in the revenge code. Stated in its simplest form, the code involved two categories of obligation: 1. 'The relationship of lord and follower involved the duty of ven-geance by the survivor if either were slain – or, at the very least, the exaction of a compensation high enough to do honour to the slain man' (Whitelock [2205.1] 31). 2. 'If a man were killed, it was the duty of his kindred to take ven-geance on the slayer of his kindred, or to exact compensation' (Whitelock, *ibid.*, 39). Just as the lord's retainers ascribed their victories to him (*e.g.*, Eofor and Wulf killed Ongentheow, but their lord Hygelac is called *bonan Ongenþeoes* 'killer of Ongentheow', *Bwf* 1968a), so the lord accepted ultimate

[27] See also *Gen* 1538b, 2037a, 2046a, 2818b, and *Dan* 311a.

responsibility for his retainers' acts of slaying, whether criminal or in war. Therefore, no matter which Frisian actually killed Hnæf, Finn bore responsibility, since he was king of the Frisians at the time of the battle. Complicating all this is Tacitus's confusing statement that among the Germans, 'to have left the field and survived one's chief . . . means lifelong infamy and shame'.[28] Although this ethical wrinkle seems to govern *The Battle of Maldon*, exceptions do occur (see Chb 278); and, as Ayres wisely notes, 'the injunction not to survive one's lord was counsel of perfection; with the best will in the world it couldn't always be managed' (Ayr 288). For example, both the British hostage and the ealdorman's godson survive the hall-fight in the *Chronicle* incident of Cynewulf and Cyneheard. The chronicler makes a point of their being severely wounded, and their excuse may be that their wounds prevented their taking vengeance (Ayr 288, *ASC* A755). In some cases, revenge might be delayed, and might come despite earlier compensation, as shown in this incident:

Earl Uhtred of Northumbria roused the enmity of Thurbrand, a member of a rich landed family in Yorkshire, and he engineered the murder of Uhtred in 1016, as he entered the hall at *Wiheal* to make his submission to Cnut. Uhtred's son Aldred avenged his father by killing Thurbrand, and the feud descended to the latter's son Carl, but by the intervention of friends a settlement was made, and mutual reparations were paid. It seemed so complete, that Aldred and Carl became sworn brothers and planned to go together on a pilgrimage to Rome; but they were hindered by a storm, and, while they were together at Carl's house at Rise, something . . . must have caused Carl to remember old grudges, for he slew Aldred in Rise wood. The feud then lay dormant for a long time. It was not until 1073,

[28] Tacitus, *Germania*, ed. and trans. W. Peterson (London: Heinemann, 1914), § XIV, pp. 284–5. But see F. Norman, 'The Early Germanic Background of Old English Verse', in D. A. Pearsall and R. A. Waldron, eds., *Medieval Literature and Civilization* (London: Athlone Press, 1969), 6, and J. M. Wallace-Hadrill, *Early Germanic Kingship in England and on the Continent* (Oxford: Clarendon Press, 1971), Chap. 1.

that Earl Waltheof, the son of Aldred's daughter, avenged his grandfather's murder by sending assassins who killed all Carl's sons and grandsons as they were feasting at the house of the eldest son, Thurbrand, at Settrington – all except two, one whom they spared for his excellent disposition, and one who was not present.[29]

The poet tells us why Finn wanted terms with Hengest:

> Wig ealle fornam
> Finnes þegnas   nemne feaum anum,
> þæt he ne mehte   on þæm meðel-stede
> wig Hengeste   wiht gefeohtan,
> ne þa wea-lafe   wige forþringan
> þeodnes ðegne.

(1080b–85a: Battle took away all of Finn's thanes except only a few, so that he could not in that meeting-place in any way fight to a conclusion the battle with Hengest, nor by fighting drive out the woe-survivors along with the prince's thane [Hengest].)

Finn's forces have been depleted to the point where they cannot fight their way into the hall or force out the Danes. The Danes, on the other hand, reduced to a wounded *wea-laf*, cannot fight their way out. Although the poet never mentions the possibility of the Frisians' burning down the hall, that option remained open to Finn and must have worried Hengest; Hnæf had considered and rejected it before: *ne her ðisse healle hornas ne byrnað*, line 4. Hengest recognizes the stalemate and offers terms, which Finn accepts.

Most critics have speculated that Hengest comes to terms because he has no choice, and that the truce arrangement runs afoul of emotion. Brodeur is eloquent here:

> It is the issue of vengeance upon which the whole situation turns. The horns of Hengest's dilemma are (1) the moral compulsion of his oath to Finn; (2) the weighty obligation which rests upon him to avenge Hnæf. Torn as he is

[29] Whitelock [2205.1] 44–5, paraphrasing *De obsessione Dunelmi*, in *Symeonis Monachi Opera Omnia*, ed. T. Arnold, Rolls Series, I (1882), 215–20.

between these conflicting obligations, he stands apart both from his own Danes and from the Germanic view of a thane's proper duty. The Danes want vengeance above all things – a desire which seems to have found vigorous expression in Guðlaf and Oslaf. To the *Beowulf*-poet's audience vengeance undoubtedly seemed the better course. The heroic code demanded vengeance. Revenge for his slain lord, and that alone, could win general approbation for Hengest. It was required of him by all proper standards of conduct – by the universal moral law (Brd 329–30).

Further:

[Hengest's] followers are on the side of the Germanic angels: one avenges one's slain lord. Hengest's tragedy resides not only in the conflict between opposed obligations, but also in the dreadful isolation into which his acceptance of peace and service with Finn had forced him. His men had agreed to those terms, but Hengest could release them; and for a long time he would not. He had become Finn's thane, but there was no happiness for him in that relationship: the blood of Hnæf lay between him and Finn. After the grim necessity which made his men acquiesce in the compact had become submerged by their desire for vengeance, Hengest's followers were separated from him by an abyss of incomprehension and mistrust; the trust and comradeship which he had shared with them were dissolved. They began to blame him for the compact, and for the dishonor which, in their minds, it had thrust upon them; they held against him his reluctance to break his pledge. Throughout the long winter of his struggle, he felt the unrelenting pressure of their reproach; and it was very hard to bear. This the poet did not need to stress; it was implicit in the means they took, through the son of Hunlaf, when their silent vigilance had made them certain that Hengest's mind was ready to respond to intervention. The interposition of the son of Hunlaf proved effective, not by convincing the hero's reason, but . . . by a last, overwhelming emotional appeal. The sight and touch of the sword proved

too much for a heart already burning to avenge. Acceptance
of the sword was a promise to Hengest's men; it restored
him to unity with them, and ended his tragic isolation
(Brodeur [231] 23–4).

Actually, as Brodeur admits ('this the poet does not need to
stress: it was implicit. . . .'), there is no textual support for the
retainers' reproach or for Hengest's 'tragic isolation'.

Most editions, presupposing that Hengest remains with
Finn all winter because the weather prevents sailing, render
lines 1127b–31 as follows:

> Hengest ða gyt
> wæl-fagne winter   wunode mid Finne
> *ea*l unhlitme;   eard gemunde,
> þeah þe *ne* meahte   on mere drifan
> hringed-stefnan;   holm storme weol,

and translate: 'Hengest still, however, stayed through that
slaughter-stained winter with Finn, very unhappily; his native
land was in his thoughts, albeit he might not guide over the
sea a ship with curved prow. The ocean heaved with storm'
(Hall translation [740] 77). If the Anglo-Saxons could not sail
in the winter, then the emendation of Ms *he* to *ne* in 1130a
is required. But they could and did in desperate conditions.
For example, *ASC* C1037 records that 'Queen Ælfgifu was
driven from the country without any mercy to face the raging
winter, and she went then to Bruges beyond the sea'. *ASC* E793
says that the vikings invaded Lindisfarne on 8 January, per-
haps an error for June; perhaps not, for the next entry cites
22 February 793. *ASC* AE874 notes that 'in this year the
[Danish] army went from Lindsey to Repton and there took
winter quarters, and drove King Burgred over this sea . . .;
he journeyed to Rome'. *ASC* AE878 begins: 'in this year the
[Danish] army stole away in midwinter after Twelfth Night
to Chippenham and rode over the West Saxon land and stayed
there and drove many of the people over the sea'; the 'sea'
may be the English Channel or the Southampton Water.
Except for the first, these few references remain too qualified
for proof, but evidence from poetry exists as well. The Sea-

farer says, 'þæt se mon ne wat þe him on foldan fægrost
limpeð, hu ic earmcearig iscealdne sæ winter wunade' (*Sfr*
12b–15: the man who fares fairest on land does not know how
I wretched-caring spent the winter on the ice-cold sea).
References to ice follow in 17a *hrimicelum* 'rime-icicles', 19a
iscaldne wæg 'ice-cold waves', and 32a *hrim hrusan bond* 'rime
bound the earth'. The Wanderer tells how he had to *hreran
mid hondum hrimcealdne sæ* 'stir [row?] with my hands the rime-
cold seas' (*Wnd* 4), and how he *wod wintercearig ofer wapema
gebind* 'travelled winter-caring over the binding of the waves',
(*Wnd* 24, and cp. 45–8, 55b–57). If the Anglo-Saxons could
not sail in the winter, these *Wanderer* and *Seafarer* references
would lose their impact. Furthermore, Northern Europe was
considerably warmer then, and modern winter conditions do
not apply. England grew wine grapes and olive trees in the
early period, and malaria was an important disease.[30] So
Hengest could sail home, as the unemended text tells us.
New punctuation produces this more satisfactory version:

> Hamas and heaburh   Hengest ða gyt
> wæl-fagne winter   wunode mid Finne
> *ea*l unhlitme   (eard gemunde),
> þeah þe he meahte   on mere drifan
> hringed-stefnan,

which may be translated, 'yet Hengest, during the slaughter-
stained winter, inhabited with Finn the houses and the high-
fortress *ea*l *unhlitme* (he thought of home), although he could
drive his ring-prowed-ship over the sea'. Parenthetical inser-
tions such as '(he thought of home)' are common constructions
in *Beowulf*; for example,

> Breca næfre git . . .
> æt heaðolace,   ne gehwæþer incer,
> swa deorlice   dæd gefremede
> fagum sweordum,   (no ic þæs fela gylpe),
> þeah ðu þinum broðrum   to banan wurde.[31]

---

[30] J. C. Russell, *Population in Europe 500–1500* (London: Fontana, 1969),
37–8.

[31] See also, *e.g.*, *Bwf* 809–12, 1316–20, 1537–8, 1612–15a, and 3053–6.

[*Bwf* 583b–87: Breca never yet . . . at battle-play, nor either of you, so boldly performed a deed with decorated swords (I do not boast much about that), although you were the killer of your brothers.] *Unhlitme*, a puzzling *hapax*, is generally taken as 'unhappily' or 'involuntarily'. Dobbie suggests that *unhlitme* 'is to be connected with *hlytm*, "casting of lots", and the related words, and means "without casting of lots"; that is, Hengest, having no choice, was forced to remain with Finn' (DbB 177). But 'without casting of lots' should produce just the opposite of 'having no choice'. Casting lots throws the result up to chance, and so *un-hlitme* should logically mean 'not by *chance*', that is 'voluntarily'. If this is true (and I think it is), if the manuscript reading *he* of 1130a is restored, and if my punctuation is accepted, a new picture of Hengest emerges. He becomes a hero remaining with Finn not because of the weather, but by his own choice, by his own design.

I interpret Hengest as waiting for his chance to avenge Hnæf. When the truce ends the battle, Hengest and Finn are evenly matched. Instead of sailing home, Hengest waits for the opportune moment to launch a surprise attack on Finn. The hesitation, the agonizing, the isolation, the tragedy of Hengest, all these are modern critical constructs, unsupported by the text.

What about the ethics of oaths and feuds? Hengest must break his oath to Finn in order to avenge Hnæf. But Finn is an enemy of the Danes and responsible for Hnæf's slaying. The unwritten code accrued certain allowances during centuries of practical application. Otto Jiriczek, commenting on the *Nibelungenlied*, says,

Germanic conceptions of good faith did not exclude crime and treachery, deceit and the breaking of oaths, for this conception was, as history and poetry show, in no wise an abstract ethical law, of general application to everyone; it first gained inner sanctity and universality through the influence of Christianity. To the Germanic warrior, keeping faith was only a matter of personal relationship, grounded in morals and manners, between peoples connected by ties of blood, marriage, hereditary or voluntary service; against enemies, whether of the family or the over-lord, or of the individual himself, bad faith, treachery, even the breaking of oaths was regarded as permissible. And so heinous treachery may accompany the highest virtue: Hagen faithlessly murders Siegfried as the avenger of his insulted lord, to whom he is faithful unto death; Kriemhilt, who attacks her own brothers, commits the crime out of fidelity to Siegfried.[32]

Hengest's treachery to Finn participates in the stratified morality of the Middle Ages; if vengeance has a superior claim over oath-keeping, then vengeance is ethical. And, Hengest proves a true and typical Dane, cast in the mould of Hrothgar, the politic king who lives twelve winters with Grendel until the avenger and his moment come.

This new version of Hengest's motives allows a revised interpretation of lines 1138b–51a. Basically I shall argue that these fourteen lines describe the steps by which Hengest rallies his forces for a surprise attack, rather than vice versa. The poet tells us in lines 1127–31a that Hengest chose to remain with Finn although he could have sailed away. After seven lines describing the winter storms and the onset of spring, which may be ascribed to the pathetic fallacy, Hengest, described as a *wrecca*, yearns (*fundode*) to leave. But he defers his departure for unfulfilled obligations. He thinks more about revenge (*gyrn-wræce*) than voyaging (*sæ-lade*). Lines 1140–1 I take as dependent on *þohte* 1139a: he wondered 'if he might bring about a *torn-gemot*, that he might bring to mind therein the sons of the giants' (*eotena, i.e.*, enemies). The *hapax legomenon torn-gemot*, meaning literally 'anger-meeting', could refer to a battle or a council. Of the twenty-one occurrences of the simplex *gemot* in the *Sprachschatz*, five refer to battles and the rest to councils. In *Soul and Body* I, 150a, *gemot-stede* refers to a council, but *hand-gemot* in *Beowulf* 1526a and 2355a and *guð-gemot* in *Genesis* 2056a and *Riddle* 15.26b refer to battles.

---

[32] Jiriczek [951] 4th ed., 49, trans. in LwB 123. For Frankish parallels, see J. M. Wallace-Hadrill, *The Long-Haired Kings* (London: Methuen, 1962), 132 and references in his note 2.

Earlier, in line 1082, the *Beowulf* poet refers to the battlefield of the first fight as a *meðel-stede*, literally, 'speaking-place'. But it is indeed a 'speaking-place', since the fight centres on the hall, where councils assemble. The lines following (1086b–1106) describe the offers of terms, so again the place involves speaking.[33] So *torn-gemot* could refer to Hengest's efforts to bring about either a battle or an angry Danish war-council which would result in a battle. More likely, it refers to both, since operationally speaking, holding such a council would be tantamount to attack. In that council, Hengest would focus support by recounting Danish grudges against the Frisians (*eotena bearn inne gemunde*).

His followers assent to his proposal symbolically when Hunlafing (whom I take to be one of Hengest's men) places a sword in Hengest's lap, and the poet assures us ironically that Hengest did not refuse such worldly advice (*ne forwyrnde worold-rædenne*). Especially ironic is the *swa* 'so' beginning this clause, since Hengest does not refuse counsel he designed in the first place. The poet then tells us the result: sword-bale fell on Finn after the final complaint voiced in the war-council, Guthlaf and Oslaf recalling the attack after the voyage to Frisia (*grimne gripe . . . æfter sæ-siðe sorge mændon*) and apportioning the blame for their woes (*ætwiton weana dæl*). The Danish *mod* overflowed, and the fatal surprise attack on Finn began.

In summary, the plot of the Finnsburh story probably runs something like this: Hoc has two children: the Danish prince Hnæf and Hildeburh, queen of the Frisian king Finn. Hnæf, accompanied by sixty retainers, including his thane Hengest, visits his sister at Finnsburh, Finn's fortress in Frisia. For reasons not stated, the Frisians attack the Danes in a hall at dawn. (Here the Fragment begins.) A Danish watchman reports an unidentified light to Hnæf, who correctly identifies it as the flashing of Frisian armour. He awakens his troop, and they rush to arm themselves and defend the doors at each end of the hall. A Frisian named Garulf urges his colleague Guthere not to risk his life against the Danes, but Guthere shouts a challenge to the defenders. Sigeferth answers from

[33] See also *Maldon* 198–201.

inside, taunting the two Frisians. The battle begins, and Garulf ironically falls first. The fight continues with Frisian casualties only. (Here the Episode begins.) Queen Hildeburh awakens to find the battle in progress, and it rages for five days in all before any Danes are killed. Hnæf and an unstated number of Danes die at the hands of the Frisian attackers. Events reach a stalemate, since Finn has insufficient forces remaining to overcome the Danes, and they in turn cannot escape from the hall. The Danes offer terms to the Frisians. Finn and Hengest swear an oath, and either pledge-money is exchanged or Hnæf's *wergild* is paid, or both. With Hildeburh presiding, the bodies of the slain, including Hnæf and Hildeburh's son, are cremated. The Frisians return to their homes. Hengest, although he thinks of home and could sail back to Denmark, chooses to remain at Finnsburh with his retainers for a peaceful, but tense winter. Spring weather tames the wild winter seas, and Hengest yearns to leave. But first he intends to avenge Hnæf. At the Danish council, Hengest receives a sword from Hunlafing, whose uncles Guthlaf and Oslaf embolden the Danish spirits by reciting all their woes since the original voyage to Frisia. The Danes attack the Frisians, kill Finn, loot Finnsburh, and carry Hildeburh back to Denmark.

IV STYLE

Most scholars consider the Fragment a 'lay', according to Campbell's definition: 'The distinction of lay and epic . . . is not a matter of relative length but of scale of treatment. Lay employs a brief technique of narrative, with compressed description and rapid conversation, while epic expands in all three fields.' Only the Fragment and the Old High German *Hildebrandslied* among surviving independent Germanic poems seem to fit this description.[34] *Judith* and *Maldon*, usually labelled as short epics, seem to satisfy as well, although their fragmentary nature makes exact determination difficult. The Fragment may be missing just a line or two at each end and

[34] Campbell [287.1], 24–5, and 16.

may be a lay, but just as likely the lost manuscript may have been one detached folio from a lost epic. If as an experiment, we ripped out a hypothetical single leaf of the *Beowulf* codex composed of folios 193v–94r, it would contain lines 2937b *wean* to 2990a *leana*, a story beginning with a siege, including a battle, and ending with a king's death, all in 54 lines, very like the scope of the Fragment.

The Episode, although part of the epic *Beowulf*, could have been derived from a lay source, for its narration is brief, its description compressed, and its conversations non-existent; and it does show a quicker tempo than the rest of *Beowulf* in general.[35] To show how unpromising genre determination can be, we may note here that the Fragment devotes its forty-eight lines to five days of combat, while the Episode describes the same fighting in 17·5 lines (1068–85a); if the Episode were expanded to the same proportions as the Fragment, it would swell to 248 lines rather than its present 90·5. In short, the epic digression Episode fits the description of a 'lay' better than the Fragment. Since both the Episode and Fragment could be either a lay or part of an epic, genre designations must remain tenuous and misleading, and generic stylistic expectations cloudy.

Several factors account for the stylistic differences of the two poems: sources of the texts and stories, psychological emphases by the two poets, and the Fragment's focus on only one-fifth of the Episode's action. The differences are in objectivity, diction, imagery, characterization, point of view, and structure.

Both narrators are objective, considered only from the standpoint of intrusions, the only exception being 37a *ne gefrægn ic*, a conventional transitional formula with no personal weight; but the Episode has a definite Danish bias, attributable to its context in Hrothgar's victory banquet (see above, pp. 12–13). Besides repeating the probably scornful epithet *eoten-*, the *scop* casts all disadvantage on the Frisians: Finn cannot drive out the Danes; Hengest initiates a truce couched in terms of what Finn must do and what Finn's troop

[35] Klb 236.

must not do, while Danish obligations remain unspecified; Finn's winter thoughts and emotions are not described; and he dies in one clause of a cataloguing sentence. On the other hand, the *Beowulf* poet also carefully refrains from denigrating the Frisians overly, since they must retain sufficient heroic stature to be worthy opponents for the Danes.

Both poets draw their diction from the conventional heroic wordhoard. Although both have roughly the same percentage of verbs (Fragment 19·9%, Episode 20%), even finite verbs (16·9%, 16·5%), the Episode has a significantly higher percentage of nouns (38·6% versus the Fragment's 29·1%), which may be a function of subject matter rather than style. Both have unusually heavy concentrations of *hapax legomena*; if, with Brodeur, we consider many *hapax legomenon* compounds as the poets' coinages, the diction shows marked originality.[36] To my taste, the Fragment's unique compounds are not particularly striking, with the exception of *guð-wudu* 5b and *ban-helm* 30a, while the Episode contains a number of intriguing unique compounds: *morþor-bealo* 1079a, *inwit-searo* 1101a, *morþor-hetes* 1105a, *wæl-fyra* 1119b and *wæl-fagne* 1128a, *ben-geato* 1121a, *lað-bite* 1122a, and *torn-gemot* 1140a.

Both poems employ conventional imagery, but with very little description of the setting; for example, although the action takes place in and around the hall of a famous king, neither poet describes it. Anglo-Saxon battle poems conventionally concentrate their attention on the events preceding combat,[37] and the Finnsburh poems are no exception. The Fragment devotes 27 of its 48 lines to preparations, while the Episode never really describes either of its two battles at all. Finn is attacked in one sentence and killed with his entire troop in one more. The Episode even excludes the ubiquitous Beasts of Battle, the *Beowulf* poet evidently reserving them for their striking allusive appearance in 3021b–27.[38] The Fragment does convey the feeling of the battle area, with its mixture of aural and visual imagery, emphasizing flashing

---

[36] Brodeur [229], chap. I, esp. pp. 33–4.
[37] *Speculum*, 44 (1969) 35–45.
[38] *Annuale Medievale*, 12 (1972) 109–10.

light and the noises of preparation and combat; but only the funeral and winter storm scenes in the Episode could be called graphic.

Neither poet devotes much attention to direct character-ization, probably because in the Episode none of the char-acters continues beyond the digression which contains them, and the Fragment's swift action makes detailed characteriza-tion inappropriate. Neither describes characters physically beyond mere epithets, a conventional technique in Old English. The Episode highlights Hildeburh in terms of her situation and emotions, and Hengest in terms of his indirectly reported thoughts. The Episode contains no direct discourse, and the poet characteristically conveys its most crucial moment (the retainers' decision to avenge Hnæf) in a gesture (Hunlafing's presentation of a sword) rather than in a speech. On the other hand, the Fragment contains 15 lines of direct discourse, and 12 more lines of speech introductions and indirect discourse (2, 18–23, 44–8); more than half of the Fragment is devoted to speaking. Hnæf's speech (3–12) char-acterizes him as an alert, perceptive leader, capable of effectively rallying his forces from a dead sleep to full readi-ness. Hnæf uses finite verbs in all but four of these twenty verses, a factor which partially accounts for the extraordinary vigour of this exhortation.[39]

Point of view controls the audience's perception of detail. Hrothgar's *scop* (and the *Beowulf* poet) narrates the Episode from an omniscient perch above the action, coupled with an emphasis on historical time. He begins by telling us the out-come of his story (1068–70), shifts to Hildeburh's emotions, contrasts Finn's former prosperity with his present predica-ment (1079b–85a), details the future truce terms in the past tense, zooms in close for the funeral, returns to his overview as he sets the weather against Hengest's plotting (1125–41), and maintains his distance throughout the council, attack, and looting. The funeral represents the high moment of pity and terror when the poet deliberately brings us in close so that the mixture of heroic and heartwrenching details becomes

[39] I am indebted to Fred Heinemann for this observation.

eþ-gesyne 'easily-seen'. The Fragment uses exactly the opposite technique: a close point of view with one drawing back to set general action against the past. The poet consistently narrates from the combatants' eye level. Lines 1–17 use close focus inside the hall, 18–23 close and outside, 24–7 close at the doors. In line 28 the viewpoint begins to draw back and the action generalizes (*Garulf* gives way to *godra fæla*) until we see all Finnsburh from a distance, flashing as if aflame (35b–36). From this viewpoint, the poet juxtaposes this battle with the Danes' earlier banquets and treasure-giving, and lets five days pass vaguely (37–42) before closing back in for a detailed view of one warrior and the *folces hyrde*'s question. When the focus is close, characters are more likely to be named on both sides, speak to one another, wield specific weapons, and suffer detailed wounds. *Maldon* and the Ongentheow episode (*Beowulf* 2922–98) display this same high verisimilitude by means of controlled point of view.

The Fragment and Episode share only one structural similarity: neither has digressions, as we might expect from their brevity. The Fragment breaks in half at line 27, when the battle preparations become actual combat. It marks its transitions by repeated conjunctions and adverbs, especially *ne*, *ac*, and *ða*, and generally endstops before shifts in the action. The Episode, on the other hand, contains a dozen incidents flowing from one to another, mostly with unified caesura transitions. For example, Hengest's stay with Finn blends into the weather imagery over a caesura at 1131a, with the synonyms *mere* and *holm* linking the sentences.

In summary, swift tempo characterizes both of these highly conventional poems. The Fragment is filled with speeches, relatively objective, stark, and graphic. The Episode is filled with thinking, biased, intense, and densely worded. In a word, the Fragment is dramatic, while the Episode broods over its themes of revenge and inexorable violence.

THE TEXTS

The edited texts which follow employ modern punctuation, capitalization, and titles, are printed in half-lines according to current practice, and have all Old English characters except *æ*, *þ*, and *ð* normalized, with editorial changes indicated by italics except for silently expanded manuscript abbreviations such as 7 > *ond, and.*

Textual variants are selective. Where I accept a previous editor's emendation, I cite the first emender and give the reading from Hickes or the *Beowulf* manuscript following a semi-colon. All textual variants appear in the glossary.

The Finnsburh Fragment

' . . . *hor*nas   byrnað næfre.'
Hleoþrode ða   hearo-geong cyning:
'Ne ðis ne dagað east*a*n;   ne her draca ne fleogeð;
ne her ðisse healle   hornas ne byrnað.
5 Ac her forþ berað.   Fugelas singað;

[1] Rgr; Hks *nas byrnað*. Some eds. add question mark after *byrnað*.
[2a] Cnb *Næfre hleoþrode*. TrF *Hnæf þa hleoþrode þa*. Hlt 1 *Ða hleoþrode*.
[2b] Trf *heaþogeorn*. Kmb 2 *heoro-geong*.
[3a] GtD; Hks *eastun*.
[5a] Etm *ac her us fyrd berað*. Grn 1 *Ac fer*. Cnb *Ac her forþ-berað*. GtD
      ferað. After 5a, some eds. insert a line: Grn 2 *feorhgeniðlan
      fyrdsearu fuslicu*. Hlt 8 *feorhgeniðlan fætte scildas*. Rgr *fyrdsearu
      rincas, fynd ofer foldan*. Bgg *fyrdsearu rincas; flacre flanbogan*. Rieger
      [1709] *fyrdsearu rincas. Nalles her on flyhte*.
[5b] TrF *swinsað*.

1] *næfre:* For metrical reasons, many eds. emend to *Hnæf*, moved to
line 2 as subject of *hleoþrode*. But line 1 seems to end a watchman's speech,
expressing doubt that the light seen is the hall gable burning. Mak regards
3-4 as a recapitulation of this speech, with the true explanation beginning
in line 5.

2] *hearo-geong* is usually emended to *heaþo-geong*, trading an intelligible
hapax legomenon for an unattested compound meaning essentially the same
thing.

2-12] The formulaic theme 'Hero on the Beach' underlies this passage,
uniting the hero Hnæf, his Danish retainers, their journey there, dawn,
Beasts of Battle, flashing weapons, and impending carnage. Cp. *Nibe-
lungenlied* 1837-49. See Crowne [421] and Fry [589].

5] *forþ berað*, from Hks *forþberað*, seems to lack an object. Many eds.
assume loss of two half-lines after 5a; see variants. Dkn, following Schilling
[1796] 116, proposes intransitive *beran*, citing *Ele* 45, *And* 1221, and NE
nautical verb 'to bear'. Klb 250 sees the weapons in 6b-7a as unexpressed
objects of *berað*, probably the best solution. In similar 'Approach to Battle'
type-scenes, bearing equipment is synonymous with advancing; see
Speculum 44 (1969) 36.

5-6] The traditional Beasts of Battle: raven and eagle (*fugelas*), and
wolf (*græg-hama*). Boer [141] 140 ff. ascribes *græg-hama* to a mail-coat, but

gylleð græg-hama. Guð-wudu hlynneð;
scyld scefte oncwyð. Nu scyneð þes mona
waðol under wolcnum. Nu arisað wea-dæda
ðe ðisne folces nið   fremman willað.

10 Ac onwacnigeað nu,   wigend mine;
habbað eowre linda;   hicgeaþ on ellen;
windað on orde; wesað onmode.'
Ða aras mænig gold-hladen ðegn;   gyrde hine his
swurde.

[6a] Mlr *Ac gylleð*.
[7b] TrF *þer*.
[9a] Rgr *ða ðe*.
[10a] TrF *Ac nu onwacnigeað*. TrB *onwæcnað*.
[11a] Bugge [272]; Hks *landa*. Kmb 1 *landa* (*æht*). Etm *handa geweald*.
      Rgr *handa gearwe*. GtB *handa*. Klg *hebbað eowre linda*. TrF *hebbað*
      eowre hlencan. Hyn 1 *hebbað eowre handa*. Thp *land*. Hlt 1 *hlencan*.
      Rieger [1709] *randas*.
[11b] Kmb 1; Hks *Hie geap*. Etm *hycgeað*. Wlk 1 *hiegeaþ*.
[12a] Thp *winnað*. TrF *standað*. Mak *þindað*.
[12b] Kmb 1; Hks *on mode*.
[13] Many eds. divide into 3 half-lines, following Cnb: Trf *Ða aras*
      [*of reste/rond-wigend*] *mænig*. Grn 2 [*rincas mine*]. Hlt 1 *Ða aras* [*of*
      ræste/rumheort] *mænig/goldhladen* [*gum*]*-ðegn*.

---

see *Wnd* 82 *hara wulf* 'grey wolf' and *Brb* 64 *græge deor* 'grey beast'. Cp.
Brb 62 *hasewan-padan* 'grey-coated', describing the eagle. But since *fugelas*
probably includes both the raven and the eagle, *græg-hama* most likely
represents the wolf. The raven appears alone in 34–5.

9] *nið:* DbM 132 translates, 'will carry out (*i.e.*, bring to fruition)
this hostility of the people', *i.e.*, Finn's troops.

11] *hiegeaþ* is usually emended to *hicgeað* after *Exo* 218 *hycgan on ellen*
'think about courage'. Wlk 1 suggests Hks *Hie geap* may be imperative of
higian 'hasten', with *on ellen* used adverbially, as in *Mld* 211b *he on ellen*
spræc 'he spoke courageously'; see *PPs* 93.2.1a, *Glc* 532b, 940b, 1026a,
1136a, 1285a. Hastening traditionally forms part of the Approach to
Battle type-scene; see *Speculum* 44 (1969) 36. But, in a private letter, Alan
Bliss objects: 'It seems to me very difficult to take *hiegeaþ* as imperative of
higian: the g in *higian* is velar, and *ge* is the regular way of spelling the palatal
sound. It would, I think, be necessary to assume that the MS had something
like *hi giaþ*, and that Hickes "improved" this to *hie geaþ*.'

12] *windað:* Early eds. read Hks *Windað* as *Þindað*, but the first letter
is *W*; cp. frontispiece *Wrecten* > *wreccea* 25a. Many recent eds. emend to
winnað, but the image reflects turning toward the vanguard at the doors.
Cp. *hwearf him on laste* 17b.

Ða to dura eodon   drihtlice cempan,
15 Sigeferð and Eaha   (hyra sword getugon),
   and æt oþrum durum   Ordlaf and Guþlaf;
   and Hengest sylf   hwearf him on laste.
   Ða gyt Garulf   Guðere styrode
   ðæt he swa freolic feorh   forman siþe
20 to ðære healle durum   hyrsta ne bær*e*,
   nu hyt niþa heard   anyman wolde;
   ac he frægn ofer eal   undearninga,
   deor-mod hæleþ,   hwa ða duru heolde.
   'Sigeferþ is min nama,' cweþ he,   'ic eom Secgena
   leod,

[15a] Mlr *Eawa.* Hlt 8 *Eah[h]a.*
[18a] TrF *Garulfe.*
[18b] Grn 1 *guðhere.* Bgg *Guðdene.* TrF *styrde.* SdV *styrede.*
[19a] Shk *hie.*
[19b] Hks *for-man.*
[20b] Etm; Hks *bæran.*
[21b] Kmb 1; Hks *Any man.*
[22a] TrF *ealle.*
[24a] Many eds. delete *cweþ he,* following Rgr.

16] *durum:* Here and at 20a, the situation demands a single door at each end of the hall; Klb 251 makes *durum* plural with singular meaning. But perhaps the hall has double doors at each end; see Cramp [402] 75, citing the progression of events in *Bwf* 721-4. See also 42b.

18] *styrode* is often emended to *styrde* to supply a verb meaning 'to restrain'. Those eds. who prefer *styrde* usually regard Guthere as restraining Garulf (often emended to *Garulfe, ds.* after *steoran*); WCh 160 notes: 'Guthere is apparently the speaker and Garulf the person who is being restrained. For it is Garulf who, neglecting the advice, falls.' But *styrian,* usually meaning 'stir up, excite', also means 'tell', as in *Bwf* 872b *snyttrum styrian* 'tell skilfully'. Hks text says, 'Then Garulf told Guthere that he should not thus bear his noble life and armour to the hall doors in the first advance, now that one hard in hostility wanted to take it away.' Ironically, Garulf the advisor falls in 31b. Both Garulf and Guthere are evidently Frisians, because one of them asks who 'holds the door', implying that he is speaking to a defender inside.

24] *cweþ he,* usually regarded as suspicious, is paralleled by *Gen* 278a *Hwæt sceal ic winnan? cwæð he,* and Old Saxon *quað he,* e.g. *Heliand* 141, 222. It may be extrametrical, a scribal insertion, or even Hks attempt at clarity.

D

25 wrec*c*ea wide cuð;   fæla ic we*a*na gebad,
    heordra hilda.   Ðe is gyt her witod
    swæþer ðu sylf to me   secean wylle.'
    Ða wæs on healle   wæl-slihta gehlyn.
    Sceolde celæs bor*d*   *c*enum on handa
30 ban-helm berstan.   Buruh-ðelu dynede,
    oð æt ðære guðe   Garulf gecrang,
    ealra ærest   eorð-buendra,
    Guðlafes sunu;   ymbe hyne godra fæla,
    hwearflicra, hwær   hræfen wandrode

[25a] Wlk 2; Hks *Wrecten*. Etm *wreccena*. Thp *wrecca*.

[25b] Kmb 1; Hks *weuna*.

[26a] Kmb 1 *heardra*.

[27a] Kmb 1 *swæ þer*.

[28a] Grn 1 *wealle*.

[29a] Shl *celod*. Etm *näglod*. Kmb 1 *cellod*. Thp *nalæs*. Hlt 1 *ceorlæs*. Hlt 3 *clæne*. Hlt 6 *celced*. Jellinek [949] *celed*.
bord] Kmb 1; Hks *borð*.

[29b] Grn 1; Hks *genumon*. GtD *genumen*.

[31a] Hyn 1 *oð þæt æt*.

[33a] Mlr *Guðulfes*. TrF *Guðheres*.

[33–4] Kmb 2 divides: *Guð-lafes sunu: ymb hyne/godra fæla hwearf/lacra hrær*. Thp divides after *hwearf*.

[34a] Hks *hwearflacra hrær*. Etm *hwearf lacra hræw*. Kmb 2 *hwearf lacra*

26] *Ðe . . . wylle:* Translate: 'to you is yet here fated which of two things [life or death, victory or defeat, *etc.*] you yourself will try to get from me', *i.e.* 'come find out which of us is fated to win'.

29–30] *Sceolde . . . berstan:* Hks gives *Sceolde celæs borð. Genumon handa*. For guesses at *celæs*, see glossary and variants; the usual emendation to *cellod* substitutes the equally desperate *hapax legomenon* from *Mld* 283a, *clufon cellod bord.*

ban-helm may be a kenning for shield, 'bone-protector', varying *bord*. Or it may literally mean 'bone-helmet'. Dkn 68 suggests a 'helmet decorated with bones', citing Germanic representations of horned helmets, such as the Torslunda plates. Cramp [402] 61, n. 17 adds that bone plates covered the ribs of the Benty Grange helmet: see her plate X.A. Translate: 'the *celæs* shield-board, the bone-protector [or bone-helmet] had to burst in the bold-one's hands'. See also *GfM* 40b *þær bord stunað* 'where boards crash'.

33] *Guðlafes sunu* is Garulf of 18a and 31b. Some eds. equate this Guthlaf with the Danish Guthlaf mentioned in 16 and 1148, assuming a Hildebrandian tragic situation where father and son fight on opposite

35 sweart and sealo-brun.   Swurd-leoma stod
swylce eal Finns-buruh   fyrenu wære.
Ne gefrægn ic næfre wurþlicor   æt wera hilde
sixtig sige-beorna   sel gebæran,
ne nefre swanas hwitne medo   sel forgyldan,

---

hrær. GtD hwearflicra hræw. Mlr hwearflicra hryre. TrF hreaw-blacra
hwearf. Shk Hwearf flacra hræfen. Thp hwearf laðra hræw. Soc hwarf
flacra hræw. Hlt 5 Hwearf flacra earn. Klb Hwearf flacra ærn. WCh
hwearf flacra hræw. Wrn hwearf blacra hræs. Hlt 2 hwearf blacra
hreas. Bgg Hwearf flacra hræw hræfen fram oðrum. Crawford [408]
hwearflicra hræs. Osborn Hwearf lacra hwær.

[34b] Shk [hungrig] wandrode. TrF wundrode. Hlt 1 weardode.

[36a] TrF Finnes buruh. Klp Finnes-buruh.

[38b] Kmb 1; Hks gebærann.

[39a] Grn 1; Hks swa noc. Rgr swetne medo. Grn 1 swanas swetne medo.
Thp sang ne hwitne medu. Hlt 5 medo[drinc]. Etm ne næfre swa nu/nacod-
um sweordum/swetne medo.

[39-40] Hlt 8 forgyldan/[hira sigedryhtne].

---

sides. But Klb 251 cites Godric and Wulfmær (Mld 187, 321; 113, 155) as
duplicating names of four different people; see Klaeber [1063] 308.
Beowulf has two heroes named 'Beowulf'. Surprisingly the name Guðlaf
does not appear in the corpus outside these three references, according to
W. G. Searle, ed. Onomasticon Anglo-Saxonicum (Cambridge: Cambridge
Univ. Press, 1897), 273.

33–5] ymbe . . . sealo-brun: 33b–34 depend on gecrang 31b. Hks Hwearf-
lacra hrær produced many emendations; most eds. today accept GtD hwearf-
licra hræw, which Mak 266 translates, 'corpses of the fleeting', 'of the mortal',
'of the dead'. In ELN 6 (1969), 241–2, I propose the present reading and
punctuation, translated, 'about him many good-ones, [many] active-ones,
where the raven circled', etc. For the uncommon mid-half-line break, see
And 223b–24, 699–700, Bwf 1706b–7a, Wnd 64b. M. Osborn, in Folklore 81
(1970), 185–94, offers hwearf lacra hwær, translated, 'around him many a
good fight [lacra] whirled where the raven wandered', or taking lacra as
'sacrifices', 'good men fall, sacrifices'. In the latter, the raven plays the role
of psychopompos waiting to carry off dead spirits; cp. Wnd 80–4.

37] Ne . . . næfre: The only narrator's intrusion in the Finnsburh
poems, but a common formula with no personal weight.

39] swanas means 'herdsmen' in all OE instances; cp. the perhaps
influential Old Norse sveinn 'boy, man, servant'. A doubtful emendation.

hwitne is often emended to swetne since mead is yellow rather than white.
But see NED, s.v. 'white', adj. 2a, 'various indefinite hues approaching
white, esp. dull or pale shades of yellow'. Cp. Bwf 1448a hwita helm, de-
scribing a golden helmet.

40 ðonne Hnæfe guldan   his hægstealdas.
    Hig fuhton fif dagas,   swa hyra nan ne feol
    driht-gesiða;   ac hig ða duru heoldon.
    Ða gewat him wund hæleð   on wæg gangan;
    sæde þæt his byrne   abrocen wære,
45 here-sceorpum hror,   and eac wæs his helm ðyrl.
    Ða hine sona frægn   folces hyrde
    hu ða wigend hyra   wunda genæson,
    oððe hwæþer ðæra hyssa. . . .

[41a] Grn 2 *fuhton* [*fromlice*]. Hlt 7 *nigon*.
[41]   Mlr *dagas forþ gerimed*/*and nihta cðer swylc.* TrF *dagas* [*ferhð-grimme
       hæleð,*/*and niht eal*]-*swa: hyra nan oðfeol.*
[41b] Hlt 5 *swa ne feol hyra nan.*
[42b] Kmb 2 *dura*
[43b] Etm *onweg.*
[45a] TrF *here-sceorp ahroren.* Thp *heresceorp unhror.*
[45b] TrF *ðyrel.*
[47]   Grn 1 *wigend*/*hyra wunda.*

43, 46] *hæleð* and *hyrde* are generally taken as Frisians, the latter being
Finn himself. However, since 43 ff. follows the statement that no Danes fell
for 5 days, this warrior may be the first downed Dane. The *folces hyrde* may
then be Hnæf asking him how the vanguard bear their wounds, or Finn
asking how his or the Danish troops fare. In a door battle, neither command-
er could see well. See Klb 252-3, Rieger [1709] 12, Bgg 28, TrB 62, Boer
[141] 147, and Greenfield, *NM*, 73 (1972) 97-102.

45] *here-sceorpum hror* modifies *hæleð* 43a, 'strong in his army-gear', or
less likely modifies *byrne* 44a, 'strong mail-shirt among his trappings'.
Notice *Bwf* 27a *felahror feran* 'journeyed very-vigorous', describing the dead
Scyld Scefing. The irony disappears in the common emendation *here-
sceorp unhror* 'weak war-gear'.

ðyrl is usually expanded to *ðyrel* for metrical reasons, although Mak re-
gards it as disyllabic: *ðyr-l.*

The Finnsburh Episode

Þær wæs sang and sweg   samod ætgædere
fore Healfdenes   hilde-wisan,
1065 gomen-wudu greted,   gid oft wrecen,
ðonne heal-gamen   Hroþgares scop
æfter medo-bence   mænan scolde:
Finnes eaferum,   ða hie se fær begeat,

[1064] Möller [1461] *ofer*. Lübke [1269] *Healfdenes [suna]*. TrF *Healf-dena*·
[1065b] Lübke [1269] *eft*.
[1067–68] Sdg 3 inserts *cwæð, him ealdres wæs ende gegongen*.
[1068a] Kmb 2 (from Thorpe) *[be] Finnes*. Trautmann [2107] *eaferan*.

1063–67] *Þær . . . scolde:* The Episode forms part of the entertainment at
Hrothgar's banquet celebrating Beowulf's victory over Grendel. For the
implications of this context, see Introduction, pp. 12–13.

Healfdenes hilde-wisan is Hrothgar, now king of the Danes. WCh
labels *hilde-wisan dp.*, 'the old captains who had fought under Healfdene'.

1067] *mænan:* Does the Episode represent the *scop*'s directly reported
words or a summary in indirect discourse, and exactly where does the
Episode begin? Green [663] summarizes the various arguments; following
Gummere's suggestion that 'the epic poet, counting on his readers' fami-
liarity with the story . . . simply gives the headings' [720] 69 n. 5, Green
concludes that these 'headings' are spoken by the *scop* and directly reported
by the poet. Girvan [637] 334 asserts that the Episode 'begins nowhere in
Beowulf; the poet passes into an individual narrative, introduced by a
string of allusions in accordance with the habitual method'. Those editors
opting for direct discourse variously begin the Episode with quotation
marks preceding *Finnes*, *hæleð*, *Hnæf*, and *Ne huru*. A summary in indirect
discourse seems more in keeping with *Beowulf*'s style (cp. 90b–98, 874b–
915), and is assumed here.

1068 *Finnes eaferum* is comitative *dp.* according to Wrn 204; translate:
'with the sons [men] of Finn, when the sudden attack came upon them
[the Frisians], the hero of the Half-Danes, Hnæf of the Scyldings, had to fall
in the Frisian-slaughter'. Most editors emend to *be Finnes*, without a preced-
ing colon, translating, 'hall entertainment concerning the sons of Finn',
DbB 170; but see A. Bliss, *The Metre of Beowulf*, 2nd ed., (Oxford: Blackwell,
1968), 46–47. Trautmann [2107] offers *eaferan*, *ap.* object with *heal-gamen*
of *mænan*; see Klaeber [1050] 443 and [1062] 370. WCh 55 makes *eaferum*

hæleð Healf-dena,   Hnæf Scyldinga,
1070 in Fres-wæle   feallan scolde.
Ne huru Hildeburh   herian þorfte
eotena treowe.   Unsynnum wearð
beloren leofum   æt þam *lind*-plegan
bearnum and broðrum;   hie on gebyrd hruron
1075 gare wunde.   Þæt wæs geomuru ides.
Nalles holinga   Hoces dohtor
meotod-sceaft bemearn,   syþðan morgen com,
ða heo under swegle   geseon meahte
morþor-bealo maga.   Þær he ær mæste heold
1080 worolde wynne,   wig ealle fornam
Finnes þegnas   nemne feaum anum,

[1069a] GtD *Healfdenes*.
[1072] Most eds. capitalize *eotena* throughout.
[1073b] Kmb 1; Ms *hildplegan*.
[1079b] Thp *heo*. *Moste* corrected to *mæste* in same hand.
[1081b] *ū* added to *fea* in same hand.

---

ip., translating, 'at the hands of the children of Finn'. Intentional poetic ambiguity could account for both senses, dative and instrumental, operating at once; Hnæf dies because of Finn's men, and eventually accompanied by them.

1071-2] *Ne . . . treowe*; Litotes, as in *Brb* 39b, 44b, and 47b; see Klaeber [1028] 414-15 and Wms 24-33, App. II. See Introduction, pp. 13-16, for interpretation of this troublesome sentence.

1074] *bearnum and broðrum*, both plural, seem to contradict 1114 ff., where Hildeburh has lost her brother Hnæf and only one son. But plurals with singular meaning occur in OE poetry; cp. *Bwf* 565b, 567a, and 1574a.

1077] *morgen:* Hildeburh awakens to find the battle raging, not ended. From 41a, we know it continued at least four more days. The poet typically mixes his time scheme here, shifting from the results of the fighting in 1068-70 to a glance at past or future or both in 1071-72a (see Introduction, pp. 13-16), and back to results in 1072b-75a. 1075b ambiguously refers to present and continuing emotions. 1076-79a refers to the first morning, and 1079b ff. to the end of the battle.

1079] Ms *he* is emended to *heo* by most recent editors, with a comma after 1079a *maga* and terminal punctuation after 1080a *wynne*, contrasting Hildeburh's former happiness with the disaster in progress. The Ms version applies the contrast to Finn, whose worldly joy directly depends on his warriors, now mostly dead.

þæt he ne mehte   on þæm meðel-stede
wig Hengeste   wiht gefeohtan,
ne þa wea-lafe   wige forþringan
1085 þeodnes ðegne.   Ac hig him geþingo budon:
þæt hie him oðer flet   eal gerymdon,
healle and heah-setl;   þæt hie healfre geweald
wið eotena bearn   agan moston;
and æt feoh-gyftum   Folcwaldan sunu

[1083]   Rgr *wiht Hengeste wið gefeohtan.*
[1085a] Brown [245] *ðegna.*
[1087b] Etm *healfne.*
[1088a] Most eds. capitalize *eotena.*

1082–85a] *þæt . . . ðegne*: Wrn 204–5 translates, 'so that he could not in
that place of strife . . . at all fight to a finish . . . the fight against Hengest
the prince's [Hnæf's] thane . . ., nor by warfare dislodge . . . the survivors of
the grievous disaster (*þa wea-lafe*)'. 1085a *peodnes ðegne* may, following
Wrn, vary 1083a *Hengeste*; see Campbell [287.1] 22, n. 1. More likely it is
ds. of accompaniment, 'dislodge the woe-remnant, along with the prince's
thane', Malone [1399] 150. The *wea-lafe* here and at 1098a are Danes.

Most editors translate *forþringan* as 'rescue, protect'. BT 1070 gives the
simplex *þringan* as transitive 'press, crowd, throng'; this coupled with the
intensive (often destructive) prefix *for-* could yield 'push out, crush utterly,
expel'. Alan Bliss suggests that *forþringan* might stand for **forþ-þringan*, with
a similar meaning. BTS 256 cites *Benedictine Rule* 115. 6 *ne seo ylde þa geogoðe
ne forþringe* 'nor will age displace youth' (A. Schöer, ed., *Die Angelsächsische
Prosabearbeitung der Benedictinerregel*, Kassel, 1885). See Brown [245] 115,
DbB 172. Brown emends to *ðegna*, translating, 'the wretched remnant of
the thanes of the prince'.

1085–94] Hoops [894] 137: '1086. *hie* the Frisians, *him* the Danes. –
ōðer flet "the other *Flett*", that is, the other, lower half of the hall. In the old
Germanic halls the benches stood lengthwise along the walls opposite each
other, with the seats of honour in the middle of both rows. The place of
honour on the North side, opposite the sun, was named in Scandinavian
ǫndvegi it æðra "the higher or the first high-seat", the one on the South side
ǫndvegi it úseðra "the lower or the second high-seat"; hence also *annat
ǫndvegi* "the other high-seat". The two benchrows were named respectively
æðri bekkr "the higher benchrow" and *úseðri bekkr* "the lower benchrow".
. . . It was thus also in other Germanic countries. The Danes, therefore,
received the "other" or "lower" side of the hall together with the "lower",
high-seat, which had been conceded to them' (trans. Martin Stevens). In
my opinion, *hig* refers to the Danes, offering terms to the Frisians (*him*).
Finn cannot drive the Danes out of the hall (1082–85a), but Hengest

1090 dogra gehwylce   Dene weorþode,
Hengestes heap,   hringum wenede,
efne swa swiðe   sinc-gestreonum
fættan goldes   swa he Fresena cyn
on beor-sele   byldan wolde.
1095 Ða hie getruwedon   on twa healfa
fæste frioðu-wære.   Fin Hengeste
elne, unflitme   aðum benemde:
þæt he þa wea-lafe   weotena dome
arum heolde;   þæt ðær ænig man
1100 wordum ne worcum   wære ne bræce;
ne þurh inwit-searo   æfre gemænden

[1097a] Grn 1 *unhlytme*. TrF *unblinne*. Mackie [1292] *unflitne*. TrB *unslawe*.

---

offers to surrender it in exchange for quarter and hospitality (see Wrn 205).
1086–7 *oðer flet* and *healle* probably do not refer to a different hall, since
Finn has no reason to have two in the same place; Hrothgar (*Bwf* 1299b–
1301) has other sleeping buildings, but not necessarily a second hall. I
take *oðer* as 'one of two' (Heusler [811] 32), *flet* as 'one of the long bench-
rows' (Klb 173 and Hoops above), and *healle* as 'hall space' (Hoops [894]
58 ff.). BT 805 gives *ryman* as 'to make room by removing one's self, yield,
give place', with the sense of retreating; cp. *ASC* CD1015 *rymdon heora
feondum* 'they retreated from their enemies'. In social contexts, *ryman* means
'to make roomy', *e.g., Bwf* 1975–6 *Hraðe wæs gerymed . . . feðegestum flet
innanweard* 'a floor was quickly vacated inside for the foot-guests'. Hengest
offers a retreat set in social terms: 'that they [the Danes] should vacate
entirely for them [the Frisians] one of the floors, hall-space and the high-
seat'. The rest of the terms require Finn in the *heah-setl* to treat them as
guests and retainers equally with the Frisians (but note the possible slur in
eotena 1088a). 1095–96a refers both to the Danish offer (1086–94) and
Finn's acceptance (1096b–1106).

1097] *elne, unflitme:* see glossary. Kock [1096] 109 'strongly and indis-
putably'; TrF 24 *elne unblinne* 'with incessant zeal'; Mackie [1292] *unflitne*
'earnestly and sincerely'.

1099b–1103] *þæt . . . wæs* refers to the Frisians, according to Wms 65–6.
Mal 158, 163, Hoops [894] 60; Klb 173 prefers the Danes, proposing that
'*þæt* 1099 denotes "upon condition that", and *þonne* 1104 "on the other
hand" '. But peace requires discretion on both sides, and *ænig man* more
likely means just what it says, everyone, Danes and Frisians. 1104–6
particularize the penalty Finn promises any peacebreaker in his troop,
probably with a like public understanding by Hengest for the Danes.

ðeah hie hira beag-gyfan   banan folgedon
ðeoden-lease,   þa him swa geþearfod wæs;
gyf þonne Frysna hwylc   frecnen spræce
1105 ðæs morþor-hetes   myndgiend wære,
þonne hit sweordes ecg   syððan scolde.
Að wæs geæfned,   and inge-gold
ahæfen of horde.   Here-Scyldinga
betst beado-rinca   wæs on bæl gearu.
1110 Æt þæm ade wæs   eþ-gesyne
swat-fah syrce,   swyn eal-gylden,
eofer iren-heard,   æþeling manig
wundum awyrded;   sume on wæle crungon.

[1106b] *syððan*] TrF *sehtan* or *seman.* Imelmann [937] *scyran.* Klaeber
      [1058] *seðan.* Hlt 3 *swyðan.* Hlt 7 *sidian.*
[1107a] GtD *ad.*
[1107b] Rosier [1734]; MS. *icge.* Bgg *ondiege.* Sdg 1 *andiege.* Sdg 3 *ondlicge.*
      Sedgefield [1893] *æðelinga.* Hlt 2 *itge.* Holthausen [865] *idge.*
[1109a] *a* added to *bedo* in same hand.

1102] *hie . . . folgedon: hie* = Danes. *Bana* labels one as responsible for
another's death, without necessarily denoting the actual killer or connoting
criminality. *Bwf* 1968a calls Hygelac *bonan Ongenþeoes* 'slayer of Ongen-
theow' because he led the war party which killed the Swedish king, although
Eofor struck the fatal blow, *Bwf* 2922–81. Despite the fact that Finn is not
necessarily the actual slayer of Hnæf, joining the Frisian king's *comitatus*
remains a shameful act, despite the circumstances and eventual motives, in
view of the revenge code. See Introduction, pp. 16–17, and *ASC* A755.

1106] *syððan scolde* seems to lack a verb, unless *syððan* or one of the textual
variants above is accepted as one. Moore [1469] suggests ellipsis, cites
parallel omissions, and translates, 'then the sword's edge should attend to
(deal with) it later'. Wrn 205 supplies 'to be'; translate: 'then afterwards it
would be the sword's edge (for him)'.

1107–8] *Að . . . horde: Að*, often emended to *ad* 'pyre', refers to both sides
of the treaty sworn above, 1086–1106. Ms *icge* has drawn many interpreta-
tions and emendations (see glossary and variants), none better than Rosier
[1734] to *inge-gold* 'native-gold', on the model of 1155a *ingesteald* 'native-
property'. 'Native-gold' in the sense of Frisian treasure, comes from Finn's
hoard, as confirmation of the oath, as *wergild* for Hnæf (Whitelock [2205]
18), as offerings for the pyre (Klb 173), or as reward for the warriors on
both sides (LwF 406, n. 22), or perhaps some combination of these.

1109] *betst beadorinca* is Hnæf, whose body rests on the pyre, ready for
burning.

Het ða Hildeburh   æt Hnæfes ade
1115 hire selfre sunu   sweoloðe befæstan,
ban-fatu bærnan,   and on bæl don.
Earme on eaxle   ides gnornode;
geomrode giddum.   Guð-rinc astah.
Wand to wolcnum   wæl-fyra mæst;
1120 hlynode for hlawe.   Hafelan multon,
ben-geato burston   ðonne blod ætspranc,
lað-bite lices.   Lig ealle forswealg,
gæsta gifrost,   þara ðe þær guð fornam
bega folces;   wæs hira blæd scacen.

· xvii ·

1125 Gewiton him ða wigend   wica neosian
freondum befeallen,   Frysland geseon.

[1117a] Thp *axe*. Boer [141] *earm ond eaxle*. Holthausen [874] *eame*.
[1118b] GtD *guðrec*. Grn 1 *guðhring, guðreoc*.
[1121b] Many eds. omit comma.

1116] *and on bæl don* should chronologically precede *ban-fatu bærnan*, but cp. the similar *hysteron proteron* in *Bwf* 2124–26 *hy hine ne moston . . . bronde forbærnan, ne on bel hladan* 'they could not burn him up with firebrands, nor load him on the pyre'. Cp. *Phx* 214b–16a.

1117] *earme on eaxle: on eaxle* probably means 'at the shoulder', *i.e.*, 'beside'; see Schröer [1830] 334. *Cp. Bwf* 358b–59a *he for eaxlum gestod Deniga frean* 'he stood before the shoulders of the Danish king' and 2853b *frean eaxlum neah* 'next to his lord's shoulders', both in the sense of 'even with'. Many editors emend to *eame on eaxle* 'at his uncle's shoulder', punctuating the phrase with the previous sentence. As punctuated here, it refers to the *ides* standing alongside the pyre, either Hildeburh or perhaps a ritual mourner and mistress of ceremonies; see M. Osborn, *Folklore*, 81 (1970), 188–9, Mustanoja [1522], and Ibn Fadlan's *Risala*, trans. in Smyser [1978]. Cp. *Bwf* 3150–52a, where a woman (Hygd?) sings sad songs over the dead Beowulf.

1118] *Guðrinc astah* is normally taken as describing the actual placing of Hnæf or Hildeburh's son on the pyre following her command in 1114–16; see Klb 174, DbB 176. Grimm [690] 262 gives 'The warrior's spirit rose into the air'; for discussion of Christian and Celtic implications of this image, see Hoffmann [832] and Osborn, *op. cit.* Cp. *Chr* 702b *godbearn astag* 'the Son of God ascended' into heaven.

1125] *Wigend*, sometimes ascribed to the Danes (Wms 78–82, Mal 158, and Malone [1328] 83–5), refers to the Frisians, since *wica neosian* generally

Hamas and hea-burh   Hengest ða gyt
wæl-fagne winter   wunode mid Finne
eal unhlitme   (eard gemunde),
1130 þeah þe he meahte   on mere drifan
hringed-stefnan.   Holm storme weol;
won wið winde.   Winter yþe beleac
is-gebinde,   oþðæt oþer com
gear in geardas,   swa nu gyt deð,
1135 þa ðe syngales   sele bewitiað
wuldor-torhtan weder.   Ða wæs winter scacen,

[1128b–29a] Klb 1; MS. *finnel un hlitme*. Kmb 2 *mid Finne/elne*. Soc *ealles*. Grn 1 *unflitme*.
[1130a] GtD *þe he* [*ne*]. Hlt 5 *þe ne*.
[1134b] Thp *doð*.
[1135a] Sedgefield [1898] *þam*.

---

means 'to go home' (DbB 176, Hoops [896] 141). Most editors punctuate *hamas and heaburh* as objects of *geseon*. Klaeber [1044] 193 interprets *heaburh* as 'their respective homes in the country'; Chb 259 n. 4 counters: 'it seems to me taking a liberty with the text to interpret *hēaburh* (singular) as the "respective homes in the country" to which Finn's warriors resort on demobilization. And the statement of *ll.* 1125–7, that the warriors departed from the place of combat to see Friesland, seems to necessitate that such place of combat was not in Friesland. . . . We are justified in arguing that Finnsburg, the site of the first battle in which Hnæf fell (from which site the warriors depart to visit Friesland and the *hēaburh*) was not identical with the *hēaburh*, and did not lie in Friesland.' DbB 177 translates *Frysland geseon* as 'visit [their homes elsewhere in] Friesland', and my new punctuation restores Finnsburh to Frisia. Translate: 'Then the warriors, deprived of friends, departed to seek their dwellings, to visit [their homes elsewhere in] Frisia. Yet Hengest during the slaughter-stained winter inhabited the houses and the high-fortress with Finn', *etc.* See *ELN* 8 (1970), 1–3.

1129–31] *eal . . . stefnan:* For interpretation, see Introduction, pp. 20–23. Translate: 'with Finn not by chance (he thought of home), although he could drive his ring-prowed ship over the sea'. Klb 175, without the parentheses in 1129b, translates the Ms reading, 'he thought longingly of his home, if . . . [speculating whether . . ., wishing for a chance to sail]'; but he emends *he* to *ne* for 'a smoother text'. Mal 158 renders, 'he longed for home, wondered whether he could drive his ring-prowed ship upon the waters'.

1133–6] *oþðæt . . . weder:* 1134a *gear* is singular, subject of *deð*; and the plural *þa ðe* refers to *weder*. DbB 178 translates, 'until another year came as

fæger foldan bearm.   Fundode wrecca,
gist of geardum.   He to gyrn-wræce
swiðor þohte   þonne to sæ-lade,
1140 gif he torn-gemot   þurh-teon mihte,
þæt he eotena bearn   inne gemunde.
Swa he ne forwyrnde   worold-rædenne,
þonne him Hunlafing   hilde-leoman,
billa selest,   on bearm dyde;
1145 þæs wæron mid eotenum   ecge cuðe.
Swylce ferhð-frecan   Fin eft begeat

[1141a] Most eds. capitalize *eotena*.
[1141b] TrF *irne*. Many eds. comma after 1141.
[1142b] Mlr *worodrædenne*. TrF *wraðrædenne*. Mal *woroldrædende*. Klaeber
       [1043] *worodrædende*.
[1143a] Bgg *Hun Lafing*.
[1145a] Most eds. capitalize *eotenum*.

---

it still does, the gloriously bright weathers which always observe the (proper) seasons'. This weather may be as much psychological as meteorological.

1137] *Fundode wrecca* describes Hengest's status as an adventurer and perhaps as a temporary exile from his home court in Denmark. *Fundian* here means 'desire, aspire, yearn' to depart (*of geardum*); see BT 349 and *Pastoral Care* 8 (ed. H. Sweet, EETS 45, p. 54, line 4) *ðonne he fundað to ðæm weorðscipe ðæs folgoðes* 'when he aspires to the honour of rule'. Many editors translate *fundode* as 'hastened, departed', assuming that Hengest actually sailed back to Denmark in the spring, to return later with avenging reinforcements, *e.g.*, LwF 415–16. But the next sentence clearly says that he chose not to sail.

1138–51] *He . . . hreþre:* For general interpretation, see Introduction, pp. 23–24.

1140–41] *gif . . . gemunde* depends on 1139a *þohte. Torn-gemot* may refer to battle or an angry Danish war-council or with intentional ambiguity to both; see Introduction, pp. 23–24. Kock [1093] 35 takes *þæt . . . inne* as a relative; Mal 158 translates, 'in which he would be mindful', *etc.* Later Kock [1108] 187–8 takes *inne* as 'darin', *i.e.*, in the battle; see Mitchell, *Neophilologus*, 52 (1968), 292–8. Wrn 207 translates, 'he was inwardly thinking'. Klb 175 admits *inne gemunde* as 'in the bottom of his heart', but prefers TrF *irne, ds.* 'iron sword'. *Inne* may perhaps be *ds.* of neuter *inn* 'dwelling, house, [here] hall', but the adverb 'therein' seems preferable. Translate: 'if he might bring about an anger-meeting, that he might bring to mind therein the sons of the giants', *i.e.*, enemies, the Frisians.

1142–5] *Swa . . . cuðe:* For summary of the Malone–Brodeur exchange on these lines, see Introduction, pp. 9–11. DbB 179–82 gives details of the

sweord-bealo sliðen   æt his selfes ham,
siþðan grimne gripe,   Guðlaf ond Oslaf
æfter sæ-siðe   sorge mændon;
1150 ætwiton weana dæl.   Ne meahte wæfre mod
forhabban in hreþre.   Ða wæs heal hroden
feonda feorum,   swilce Fin slægen,

[1151b] Bugge [272] *roden.*

---

extensive controversy over this passage. Heinzel [774] 226–7 suggests that
Hengest is stabbed, Ayr 292 that the sword is part of the followers' egging
Hengest to avenge Hnæf, and Girvan [637] 350 that 'Hunlafing' is Hengest
himself, who girds the sword on his own lap. For parallel ceremonies, see
R. F. Leslie, ed., *The Wanderer* (Manchester: Manchester Univ. Press,
1966), 74–5 and perhaps *Bwf* 2194. I interpret the gesture as the retainers'
acceptance of Hengest's plan to attack Finn. Translate: 'So he [Hengest]
did not refuse worldly-obligation, when Hunlafing put in his lap the battle-
light, best of swords; its edges were known among the giants', *i.e.*, enemies,
perhaps also punning on the traditional wonder at the excellence of *giganta
geweorc* 'work of giants'.

Hilde-leoman may be the sword's name, 'Battle-Flame', but cp. Fragment
35b *swurd-leoma.*

1146–50a] *ferhð-frecan* refers to Finn. Guthlaf and Oslaf are Danes,
probably the Guthlaf and Ordlaf of Fragment 16. Many editors assign
1149a *sæ-siðe* to a return voyage, either to or from Denmark, usually
assuming that 1137b *fundode* means the Danes actually sailed away; Guthlaf
and Oslaf would then make a report at home and return with reinforce-
ments. See Wrn 207, Mal 169, and LwF 428–9; in opposition, see my note
on 1137 above. But more likely, *sæ-siðe* is the original voyage to Frisia; see
Klb 232 n. 2, Ayr 293 n. 20. *Grimne gripe* and *sorge* are objects of *mændon*,
representing Guthlaf and Oslaf's complaints in Hengest's war-council.
Translate: 'so afterwards cruel sword-death befell deadly-daring Finn at
his own home, after Guthlaf and Oslaf lamented the savage attack and
sorrow following their [original] sea-voyage; they ascribed blame for that
share of woes' to Finn.

1150–1] *mod* may refer to Guthlaf and Oslaf (Bugge [272] 295), to
Hengest and all the Danes (Ayr 294), to the Danes at home, assuming a
voyage there (Mal 159), or to Finn's inability to keep his spirit from depart-
ing as he dies (Wms 102). Most likely it describes the battle rage Hengest
inspires in his Danes at the war-council.

1151] Ms *hroden,* usually emended to *roden* to avoid double alliteration in
the off-verse, preserves the grim irony of a hall 'decorated' by being strewn
with Frisian bodies, part of the Danish bias of the Episode. Seven lines
later the scene returns to Hrothgar's freshly decorated hall. Cp. *Bwf*
934b–35a *blode fah/husa selest* 'best of houses, adorned with blood'.

cyning on corþre,   and seo cwen numen.
Sceotend Scyldinga   to scypon feredon
1155 eal in-gesteald   eorð-cyninges
swylce hie æt Finnes ham   findan meahton
sigla, searo-gimma.   Hie on sæ-lade
drihtlice wif   to Denum feredon,
læddon to leodum.   Leoð wæs asungen,
1160 gleo-mannes gyd.

SELECT BIBLIOGRAPHY

Bracketed numbers at the end of entries refer to entries in the Bibliography cited under I. Abbreviations used in the present edition are printed in quotation marks at the end of appropriate entries.

I BIBLIOGRAPHICAL LISTS

1969   D. Fry, *Beowulf and the Fight at Finnsburh: A Bibliography* (Charlottesville). Supersedes bibliographies in Chambers [307] and Klaeber [1026].

II MANUSCRIPTS

1705   H. Wanley, Book II of Hickes [818]. [2163]
1930   M. R. James and C. Jenkins, *A Descriptive Catalogue of the Manuscripts in the Library of Lambeth Palace* (Cambridge).
1957   N. R. Ker, *Catalogue of Manuscripts Containing Anglo-Saxon* (Oxford). [1000]
1958   J. Zupitza, *Beowulf, Reproduced in Facsimile*, 2nd ed., revised by N. Davis (London). [2278]
1963   K. Malone, *The Nowell Codex: British Museum Cotton Vitellius A. XV, Second MS* (Copenhagen). [1371]

III EDITIONS

1705   G. Hickes, *Linguarum Veterum Septentrionalium Thesaurus* (Oxford). Wanley [2163] is Book II. 'Hks' [818]
1814   J. J. Conybeare, 'The Battle of Finsborough', in *Brydges' British Bibliographer* **IV,** 261–7 (London). 'Cnb' [355]
1820   N. F. S. Grundtvig, **Bjowulfs Drape* (Copenhagen). 'GtD' [707]
1826   J. J. Conybeare, *Illustrations of Anglo-Saxon Poetry*, ed. by W. D. Conybeare (London). [356]

1833   J. M. Kemble, *The Anglo-Saxon Poems of Beowulf, The Travellers Song, and The Battle of Finnesburh* (London). 'Kmb 1'
2nd ed., 1835. 'Kmb 2' [989]

1847   F. Schaldemose, *Beo-wulf og Scopes Widsið to Angelsaxiske Digte* (Copenhagen). 'Shl' [1787]

1849   L. Klipstein, *Analecta Anglo-Saxonica* (New York). 'Klp' [1078]

1850   L. Ettmüller, *Engla und Seaxna Scopas und Bōceras* (Quedlinburg and Leipzig). 'Etm' [550]

1855   B. Thorpe, *The Anglo-Saxon Poems of Beowulf, The Scop or Gleeman's Tale, and the Fight at Finnesburg* (Oxford). 'Thp' [2084]

1857   C. W. M. Grein, *Bibliothek der angelsächsischen Poesie* **1**, 255–343 (Göttingen). 'Grn 1' [675]

1861   N. F. S. Grundtvig, *Beowulfes Beorh eller Bjovulfs-Drapen* (London and Copenhagen). 'GtB' [704]

1861   M. Rieger, *Alt- und angelsächsisches Lesebuch nebst Altfriesischen Stücken* (Giessen). 'Rgr' [1705]

1863   M. Heyne, *Beowulf: Mit ausführlichem Glossar* (Paderborn). 'Hyn' [815]
5th ed., revised by A. Socin (Paderborn and Münster, 1888). 'Soc'

1867   C. W. M. Grein, *Beovulf, nebst den Fragmenten Finnsburg und Waldere* (Kassel and Göttingen). 'Grn 2' [676]

1879   R. P. Wülker, *Kleinere angelsächsische Dichtungen* (Halle and Leipzig). 'Wlk 1' [2264]

1881   R. P. Wülker, *Beowulf: Text nach der Handschrift* (Kassel). Revision of Grein [675]. 'Wlk 2' [2259]

1883   H. Möller, *Das altenglische Volksepos in der ursprünglichen strophischen Form* (Kiel). 'Mlr' [1460]

1883   R. P. Wülker, *Das Beowulfslied* (Kassel). Revision of Grein [675]. [2260]

1902   F. Kluge, *Angelsächsisches Lesebuch*, 3rd ed. only (Halle). 'Klg' [1080]

1903   M. Trautmann, 'Finn und Hildebrand', *Bonner Beiträge*, **7**, 1–64. 'TrF' [2109]

1904   M. Trautmann, *Das Beowulflied* (Bonn). 'TrB' [2106]

1905/6   F. Holthausen, *Beowulf nebst dem Finnsburg-Bruchstück*, 2 vols., (Heidelberg). 8th ed., 1948. 'Hlt' [845]

1910   W. J. Sedgefield, *Beowulf* (Manchester). 3rd ed., 1935. 'Sdg' [1892]

1914   A. J. Wyatt, *Beowulf*, revised ed. by R. W. Chambers (Cambridge). 2nd ed., 1920. 'WCh' [2267]

1915   B. Dickins, *Runic and Heroic Poems of the Old Teutonic Peoples* (Cambridge). 'Dkn' [475]

1917   W. S. Mackie, 'The Fight at Finnsburg', *JEGP* **16**, 250–73. 'Mak' [1289]

1919   L. L. Schücking, *Kleines angelsächsisches Dichterbuch* (Cöthen). 'Shk' [1851]

1920   R. Imelmann, *Forschungen zur altenglischen Poesie* (Berlin). [936]

1922   F. Klaeber, *Beowulf and the Fight at Finnsburg* (Boston). 3rd ed. with two supplements, 1950. 'Klb' [1026]

1922   W. J. Sedgefield, *An Anglo-Saxon Verse-Book* (London and Manchester). 'SdV' [1891]

1942   E. V. K. Dobbie, 'Finnsburg' in his *Anglo-Saxon Minor Poems* (New York). Anglo-Saxon Poetic Records VI. 'DbM' [481]

1953   E. V. K. Dobbie, *Beowulf and Judith* (New York). Anglo-Saxon Poetic Records IV. 'DbB' [480]

1953   C. L. Wrenn, *Beowulf with the Finnesburg Fragment* (London and Boston). 2nd ed., London, 1958. 'Wrn' [2244]
       3rd ed., revised by W. F. Bolton (London and New York, 1973). 'Blt'

IV TRANSLATIONS

1909   F. B. Gummere, *The Oldest English Epic* (New York). [720]

1927   R. K. Gordon, *Anglo-Saxon Poetry* (London and New York). [652]

1940   C. W. Kennedy, *Beowulf. The Oldest English Epic* (London, New York and Toronto). [997]

1950   J. R. C. Hall, *Beowulf and the Fight at Finnsburg: A*

E

Translation into Modern English Prose, revised ed. by
C. L. Wrenn, preface by J. R. R. Tolkien (London).
[740]

1965   K. Crossley-Holland, 'The Finnesburh Fragment', in
B. Mitchell (ed.), *The Battle of Maldon and Other Old
English Poems* (London and New York). [420]

1966   E. T. Donaldson, *Beowulf* (New York). [485]

V STUDIES

1849   J. L. K. Grimm, 'Über das Verbrennen der Leichen',
*Abhandlungen der philol.–hist. Klasse der königl. Akademie der
Wissenschaften zu Berlin*, 191–274. [690]

1864   M. Heyne, *Ueber die Lage und Konstruction der Halle
Heorot im angelsächsischen Beowulfliede: Nebst einer Ein-
leitung über angelsächsischen Burgenbau* (Paderborn).
[817]

1868–9   S. Bugge, 'Spredte iagttagelser vedkommende de
oldengelska digte om *Beowulf* og *Waldere*', *Tidskrift for
Philologi og Paedagogik*, **8,** 40–78, 287–307. [272]

1871   M. Rieger, 'Zum *Beowulf*', *ZDP*, **3,** 381–416. [1708]

1873   S. Bugge, 'Zum *Beowulf*', *ZDP*, **4,** 192–224. [274]

1884   R. Heinzel, untitled review of Möller [1460], *AfdA*,
10, 215–39. [774]

1884–5   R. P. Wülker, *Grundriss zur Geschichte der angelsächsis-
chen Litteratur* (Leipzig). [2263]

1886   H. Schilling, 'Notes on the Finnsaga. I and II', *MLN*,
1, 89–92, 116–117. [1796]

1887   S. Bugge, 'Studien über das Beowulfepos', *Beiträge*, **12,**
1–112, 360–75. 'Bgg' [273]

1889   T. Miller, 'The position of Grendel's arm in Heorot',
Anglia, **12,** 396–400. [1450]

1889   H. Möller, untitled review of B. A. K. Ten Brink,
E. Martin and E. Schmidt (eds.), *Beowulf: Unter-
suchungen* (London and Strasbourg), *ESt*, **13,** 247–315.
[1461]

1891   M. H. Jellinek, 'Zum *Finnsburgfragment*', *Beiträge*, **15,**
428–31 [949]

1891   A. Schröer, 'Zur Texterklärung des *Beowulf*', *Anglia*,
        13, 333-48. [1830]

1891-2 P. J. Cosijn, *Aanteekeningen op den Beowulf* (Leiden).
        [389]

1892   F. Holthausen, 'Zur Textkritik altenglischer Dich-
        tungen', *Beiträge*, **16,** 549-52. [874]

1893   H. Lübke, untitled review of Cosijn [389], *AfdA*, **19,**
        341-2. [1269]

1894   R. Kögel, *Geschichte der deutschen Litteratur bis zum
        Ausgange des Mittelalters* (Strasbourg). [1110]

1897   E. A. Kock, *The English Relative Pronouns* (Lund).
        [1093]

1898   O. L. Jiriczek, *Die Deutsche Heldensage* (Strasbourg),
        trans. by M. G. Bentinck-Smith, *Northern Hero Legends*
        (London, 1902). 4th ed., Berlin and Leipzig, 1913.
        [951]

1899   M. Trautmann, '*Berichtigungen, Vermutungen und Er-
        klärungen zum Beowulf: Erste Hälfte*', *Bonner Beiträge*, **2,**
        121-92. [2107]

1902   F. Holthausen, 'Zum *Beowulf*', *Beiblatt zur Anglia*, **13,**
        363-4. [865]

1902   F. Klaeber, 'Zum *Beowulf*', *Archiv*, **108,** 368-70. [1062]

1903   A. Olrik, *Danmarks Heltedigtning:* I. *Rolf Krake og den
        ældre Skjoldungrække* (Copenhagen). Translated and
        revised by Olrik and L. M. Hollander, *The Heroic
        Legends of Denmark* (New York, 1919). [1587]

1903-4 R. C. Boer, 'Finnsage und Nibelungensage', *ZDA*,
        47, 125-60. [141]

1905   T. von Grienberger, untitled review of Heyne [815],
        7th ed., *Zeitschrift für die österreichischen Gymnasien*, **56,**
        744-61. [682]

1905   F. Klaeber, 'Bemerkungen zum *Beowulf*', *Archiv*, **115,**
        178-82. [1020]

1905   F. Klaeber, 'Notizen zur Texterklärung des *Beowulf*',
        Anglia, **28,** 439-47. [1050]

1905   M. Trautmann, 'Nachträgliches zu Finn und Hilde-
        brand', *Bonner Beiträge*, **17,** 122. [2110]

1905–6   M. Rieger, 'Zum Kampf in Finnsburg', *ZDA*, **48**, 9–12. [1709]

1907   H. M. Chadwick, *The Origin of the English Nation* (Cambridge). [303]

1907   F. Klaeber, 'Minor Notes on the *Beowulf*', *JEGP*, **6**, 190–6. [1044]

1908   F. Klaeber, 'Zum *Finnsburg-Kampfe*', *ESt*, **39**, 307–8. [1063]

1909   R. Imelmann, untitled review of Heyne [815]; 8th ed., revised by L. L. Schücking, *Deutsche Literaturzeitung*, **30**, 995–1000. [937]

1909   F. Klaeber, 'Textual notes on the *Beowulf*', *JEGP*, **8**, 254–9. [1058]

1910   T. von Grienberger, 'Bemerkungen zum *Beowulf*', *Beiträge*, **36**, 77–101. [680]

1910   W. J. Sedgefield, 'Notes on *Beowulf*', *MLR*, **5**, 286–8. [1898]

1912   R. W. Chambers, *Widsith: A Study in Old English Historical Legend* (Cambridge). [315]

1912   H. Falk, 'Altnordisches Seewesen', *Wörter und Sachen*, **4**, 1–122. [557]

1912   K. Stjerna, *Essays on Questions Connected with the Old English Poem of Beowulf*, ed. and trans. by J. R. C. Hall (Coventry). [2018]

1915   F. Klaeber, 'Observations on the Finn Episode', *JEGP*, **14**, 544–9. [1051]

1915   W. W. Lawrence, '*Beowulf* and the tragedy of Finnsburg', *PMLA*, **30**, 372–431. 'LwF' [1190]

1916   A. Green, 'The Opening of the Episode of Finn in *Beowulf*', *PMLA*, **31**, 759–97. [663]

1917   N. S. Aurner, *An Analysis of the Interpretations of the Finnsburg Documents* (Iowa City). [44]

1917   H. M. Ayres, 'The tragedy of Hengest in *Beowulf*', *JEGP*, **16**, 282–95. 'Ayr' [48]

1917   L. M. Hollander, '*Beowulf* 33', *MLN*, **32**, 246–7. [836]

1918   E. A. Kock, 'Interpretations and emendations of early English texts: IV', *Anglia*, **42**, 99–124. [1096]

1919 C. Brett, 'Notes on passages of Old and Middle English', *MLR*, **14,** 1–9. [212]

1919 C. F. Brown, '*Beowulf*, 1080–1106', *MLN*, **34,** 181–3. [245]

1919 S. Moore, '*Beowulf* notes', *JEGP*, **18,** 205–16. [1467]

1920 G. Neckel, '*Die Überlieferungen vom Gotte Balder dargestellt und vergleichend untersucht* (Dortmund). [1550]

1921 N. S. Aurner, *Hengest: A Study in Early English Hero Legend* (Iowa City). [45]

1921 K. Schreiner, *Die Sage von Hengest und Horsa: Entwicklung und Nachleben bei den Dichtern und Geschichtsschreibern Englands* (Berlin). [1822]

1921 W. J. Sedgefield, 'Miscellaneous notes: suggested emendations in Old English texts', *MLR*, **16,** 59. [1897]

1922 A. Heusler, untitled review of Imelmann [936], *AfdA*, **41,** 27–35. [811]

1922 W. S. Mackie, 'The Fight at Finnsburg', *MLR*, **17,** 288. [1290]

1923 E. A. Kock, untitled review of Klaeber [1026], 1st ed., *ANF*, **39,** 185–9. [1108]

1923 K. Malone, *The Literary History of Hamlet: I. The Early Tradition* (Heidelberg). [1353]

1924 S. J. Crawford, untitled review of Sedgefield [1891], *MLR*, **19,** 104–8. [408]

1924 R. A. Williams, *The Finn Episode in Beowulf: An Essay in Interpretation* (Cambridge). 'Wms' [2221]

1925 H. C. Wyld, 'Diction and imagery in Anglo-Saxon poetry', *Essays and Studies*, **11,** 49–91. [2270]

1926 K. Malone, 'Danes and Half-Danes', *ANF*, **42,** 234–40. [1320]

1926 K. Malone, 'The Finn Episode in *Beowulf*', *JEGP*, **25,** 157–72. 'Mal' [1326]

1926 K. Malone, untitled review of Williams [2221], *JEGP*, **25,** 114–17. [1402]

1928 K. Malone, 'Hunlafing', *MLN*, **43,** 300–304. [1341]

1928 K. Malone, untitled review of Lawrence [1188], *Speculum*, **3,** 612–15. [1405]

1928–34   H. Schneider, *Germanische Heldensage* (Berlin and Leipzig). [1813]

1929   K. Malone, 'Notes on *Beowulf:* I', *Anglia*, **53,** 335–6. [1363]

1929   S. Moore, 'Notes on *Beowulf*', in K. Malone and M. B. Ruud (eds.), *Studies in English Philology: A Miscellany in Honor of Frederick Klaeber* (Minneapolis). [1469]

1930   W. W. Lawrence, *Beowulf and the Epic Tradition*, reprinted with minor alterations (Cambridge, Mass.). 'LwB' [1188]

1931   H. F. Scott-Thomas, '*The Fight at Finnsburg:* Guthlaf and the son of Guthlaf', *JEGP*, **30,** 498–505. [1886]

1932   F. Holthausen, 'Zu *Finsburg* v. 36', *Beiblatt zur Anglia*, **43,** 256. [862]

1932   J. Hoops, *Beowulfstudien* (Heidelberg). [894]

1932   J. Hoops, *Kommentar zum Beowulf* (Heidelberg). [896]

1932   F. Klaeber, 'Garulf, Guthlafs Sohn, im *Finnsburg-Fragment*', *Archiv*, **162,** 116–17. [1038]

1932   F. Klaeber, 'Eine kleine Nachlese zum *Beowulf*', *Anglia*, **56,** 421–31. [1043]

1932   W. J. Sedgefield, 'Emendations of the *Beowulf* text', *MLR*, **27,** 448–51. [1893]

1933   K. Malone, untitled review of Hoops [896], *English Studies*, **15,** 149–51. [1399]

1933   W. J. Sedgefield, 'The Finn Episode in *Beowulf*', *MLR*, **28,** 480–2. [1894]

1934   J. O. Beaty, 'The echo-word in *Beowulf* with a note on the *Finnsburg Fragment*', *PMLA*, **49,** 365–73. [78]

1933   H. Schneider, *Englische und nordgermanische Heldensage* (Berlin). [1811]

1935–6   K. Malone, 'Healfdene', *ESt*, **70,** 74–6. [1337]

1938   C. F. Brown, '*Beowulf* and the *Blickling Homilies* and some textual notes', *PMLA*, **53,** 905–16. [246]

1938   F. Holthausen, untitled review of Sedgefield [1892], 3rd ed., *Literaturblatt für germanische und romanische Philologie*, **59,** (1938), 163–7. [887]

1938   K. Malone, '*Widsith* and the critic', *ELH*, **5,** 49–66.

1938 G. Sanderlin, 'A note on *Beowulf* 1142', *MLN*, **53**, 501–3. [1760]

1939 F. Klaeber, 'Beowulfiana Minora', *Anglia*, **63**, 400–25. [1028]

1939 W. S. Mackie, 'Notes upon the text and the interpretation of *Beowulf*', *MLR*, **34**, 515–24. [1292]

1940 R. Girvan, 'Finnsburuh', *Pr. of the British Academy*, **26**, 327–60. 'Grv' [637]

1940–1 F. Holthausen, 'Zu altenglischen Dichtungen', *ESt*, **74**, 324–8. [855]

1943 A. G. Brodeur, 'The climax of the Finn Episode', *Univ. of California Publications in English*, **3**, 285–361. 'Brd' [230]

1943 A. G. Brodeur, 'Design and motive in the Finn Episode', *Univ. of California Publications in English*, **14**, 1–42. [231]

1943 K. Malone, 'Hildeburg and Hengest', *ELH*, **10**, 257–84. [1338]

1945 K. Malone, 'Finn's stronghold', *Modern Philology*, **43**, 83–5. [1328]

1945 K. Malone, 'On *Finnsburg* 39', *Review of English Studies*, **21**, 126–7. [1376]

1949 G. R. Ward, 'Hengest', *Archaeologica Cantiana*, **61**, 77–135. [2164]

1950 A. Bonjour, *The Digressions in Beowulf* (Oxford). [159]

1952 D. Whitelock, *The Beginnings of English Society* (London and Baltimore). [2205.1]

1957 R. Cramp, 'Beowulf and archaeology', *Medieval Archaeology*, **1**, 55–7. Reprinted in D. Fry, (ed.), *The Beowulf Poet* (Englewood Cliffs, 1968). [402]

1958 D. Whitelock, *The Audience of Beowulf*, corrected ed. (Oxford). [2205]

1959 A. G. Brodeur, *The Art of Beowulf* (Berkeley). [229]

1959 R. W. Chambers, *Beowulf, An Introduction*. 3rd. ed. with supplement by C. L. Wrenn (Cambridge). 'Chb' [307]

1959 K. Malone, 'The Finn Episode once again', in *Festschrift für Walter Fischer, zu seinem 70. Geburtstag* (Heidelberg), 1–3. [1327]

1960   D. K. Crowne, 'The hero on the beach: An example of composition by theme in Anglo-Saxon poetry', *NM*, **61**, 362–72. [421]

1962   A. Campbell, 'The Old English epic style', in N. Davis and C. L. Wrenn (eds.), *English and Medieval Studies Presented to J. R. R. Tolkien* (London). [287.1]

1962   K. Malone, *Widsith*, 2nd ed. (Copenhagen). 'MlW' [1393]

1965   S. B. Greenfield, *A Critical History of Old English Literature* (New York; published in London, 1966). [670]

1965   R. L. Hoffman, 'Guðrinc astah: *Beowulf* 1118b', *JEGP*, **64**, 660–7. [832]

1965   H. M. Smyser, 'Ibn Fadlān's Account of the Rūs with some commentary and some allusions to *Beowulf*', in J. B. Bessinger and R. P. Creed (eds.), *Franciplegius; Medieval and Linguistic Studies in Honor of Francis Peabody Magoun, Jr.* (New York). [1978]

1966   D. Fry, 'The hero on the beach in *Finnsburh*', *NM*, **67**, 27–31.

1966   J. L. Rosier, '*Icge Gold* and *Incge Lafe* in *Beowulf*', *PMLA*, **81**, 342–6. [1734]

1967   R. E. Kaske, 'The *Eotenas* in *Beowulf*', in R. P. Creed (ed.), *Old English Poetry, Fifteen Essays* (Providence).

1967   K. Malone, 'The Old English Period', in A. C. Baugh (ed.), *A Literary History of England*. 2nd ed. (New York and London). [1375]

1967   T. F. Mustanoja, 'The unnamed woman's song of mourning over Beowulf and the tradition of ritual lamentation', *NM*, **68**, 1–27. [1522]

1967   C. L. Wrenn, *A Study of Old English Literature* (New York). [2247.1]

1968   R. L. S. Bruce-Mitford, *The Sutton Hoo Ship–Burial, A Handbook* (London). [251]

1968   B. Mitchell, 'Two syntactical notes on *Beowulf*', *Neophilologus*, **52**, 292–8.

1968   H. Ringbom, *Studies in the Narrative Technique of Beowulf and Lawman's Brut* (Åbo).

1969 D. Fry, '*Finnsburh* 34a: *Hwearflicra Hwær*', *ELN*, **6,** 241–2.

1969 D. Fry, 'Themes and type-scenes in *Elene* 1–113', *Speculum*, **44,** 35–45.

1970 D. Fry, 'The location of Finnsburh: *Beowulf* 1125–29a', *ELN*, **8,** 2–3.

1970 M. Osborn, 'The Finnsburg raven and *Guðrinc Astah*', *Folklore*, **81,** 185–94.

1971 R. Girvan, *Beowulf and the Seventh Century*, reissued with a new chapter by R. L. S. Bruce-Mitford (London). [636]

1972 D. Fry, 'Type-scene composition in *Judith*', *Annuale Medievale*, **12,** 100–19.

1972 S. B. Greenfield, ' "Folces Hyrde", *Finnsburh* 46B', *NM*, **73,** 97–102

GLOSSARY

This concordance-glossary lists words under the forms occurring in the texts, except that nouns and adjectives appear under the nominative singular and verbs under the infinitive (except 'to be', which is under *eom*). All forms are cross-referenced unless they adjoin the headword. The order of letters is strictly alphabetical. Æ is treated as a separate letter following *a*. Þ and Ð are normalized, so that *þ* is employed at the beginning of a word or element of a compound, but *ð* in other positions; *þ* and *ð* follow *t*. The alphabetizing ignores the prefix *ge-*.

Abbreviations are standard; *v* and *wv* represent strong and weak verbs respectively, with classes in Arabic numerals. ‡ signifies a *hapax legomenon*. † a form found only in poetry, an * a reconstructed form not attested in the corpus. After entries for compounds, the symbols 1P, 2P BP, and NP represent 'first element poetic', 'second element poetic', 'both elements poetic', and 'neither element poetic' respectively.

References to *New English Dictionary* headwords are printed in capital letters; words not the true phonological descendant of the Old English form appear in italic capitals. Brackets enclose *NED* headwords which are obsolete, archaic, or radically different in meaning. Line number references following forms are complete, and those marked *V* refer to variant forms. *H* signifies a reading from Hickes's text, and *MS* the reading in Cotton Vitellius A. XV.

The entries attempt to convey the range of meanings of a word in the Old English language as a whole, and some include commentary on literary connotations where they can be determined. The reader should select the meaning most appropriate for the context, while keeping the other possibilities in mind. Compounds, including names, are defined literally, with second elements cross-referenced.

A

ābrecan, *v.(4),* [ABREAK]; conquer, capture, violate, destroy: *pp.* **abrocen** 44.

ac, *conj.,* [AC]; but: 5, 6V, 10, 22, 42, 1085.

ād, *m.a-stem,* [AD]; pyre, fire: *ns.* 1107V; *ds.* **-e** 1110, 1114.

āgan, *ppv.(7);* OWN, have: *inf.* 1088.

āhebban, *v.(6),* [AHEAVE]; raise, take: *pp.* **ahæfen** 1108.

āhrēosan, *v.(2),* [REOSE]; RUSH,

fall: *pp.* **ahroren** damaged (TrF *beschädigt*) 45V.

ān, *num., adj.:* ONE, only: *dpm.* **fēaum ānum** only a few 1081.

and, *conj.;* AND: 15, 16, 17, 35, 41V, 45, 1063, 1074, 1087, 1089, 1107, 1116, 1117V, 1127, 1148, 1153. Invariably *and* in Hks; all others 7 except 1117V, 1148 *ond*.

***andīege,** *adv.,* openly (Gothic *andaugjo*) or *adj.* confronting the

eye, ready: 1107V. See **ondiege**
and Sdg 1.

ānyman, *v.(4)*, [NIM, ANIM]; take
away, deprive of: *inf.* 21. See
for-niman.

ār, *f.ō-stem*, [ORE]; honour, respect,
kindness, mercy: *dp.* **-um** 1099.

ārīsan, *v.(1)*; ARISE, rise: *pres.3p.*
ārīsað 8; *pret.3s.* **ārās** 13.

asce, *f.n-stem*; ASH, ashes, dust:
ds. **axe** 1117V.

āsingan, *v.(3)*; SING to a conclusion,
deliver, compose: *pp.* **āsungen**
1159. See **singan**.

āstāh, see **āstīgan**.

āstīgan, *v.(1)*, [ASTY]; ascend, rise:
pret.3s. **āstāh** 1118.

āð, *m.a-stem*; OATH: *ns.* 1107; *dp.*
-um 1097.

āwyrdan,   *wv.(1b)*,   [WERDE];
spoil, injure, destroy, kill: *pp.*
āwyrded 1113.

axe, see **asce**.

Æ

†**æfnan**, *wv.(1b)*, perform, fulfil,
carry out: *pp.* **geæfned** pre-
pared 1107.

ǣfre, *adv.*: EVER: 1101.

æfter, *prep.w.dat.*, along, among,
through: 1067; AFTER 1149.

æht, *f.i-stem*, [AUGHT]; possession,
power: *as.* 11V.

ǣnig, *adj.*, *pron.*; ANY: 1099.

ǣr, *adv.*, [ERE]; before, previously:
1079; *supl.* **ǣrest** first 32.

ærn, see **earn**.

æt, *prep.w.dat.*; AT: 16, 31, 37,
1073, 1110, 1114, 1147, 1156.

ætgædere, *adv.*, [GATHER]; toge-
ther: 1063.

‡**ætspringan**, *v.(3)*, [ATSPRING];
out-spring, flow, spurt: *pret.3s.*
ætspranc 1121.

ætwītan, *v.(1)*, *w.acc. of thing*,
[ATWITE]; blame (someone for

something),   taunt: *pret.3p.*
ætwiton 1150.

æðeling, *m.a-stem*, [ATHELING];
prince, noble, hero, man: *ns.*
1112; *gp.* **-a** 1107V.

B

bana, *m.n-stem*, [BANE]; slayer: *ds.*
banan 1102. Not necessarily
connoting 'murderer'; see Chb
251.

†**bān-fæt**, *n.a-stem*, [BONE + FAT];
bone-vessel, *i.e.*, body, corpse:
ap. **bān-fatu** 1116. NP.

‡**bān-helm**, *m.a-stem*; BONE-HELMET,
-protector: *ns.* 30. Kenning for
shield? Dkn suggests 'helmet
decorated with bones', and cp.
Bwf 780 *bānfāg* 'bone-adorned'.
See Stjerna [2018] 8 and **helm**.
NP.

bǣl, *n.a-stem*, [BALE]; fire, pyre:
as. 1109, 1116.

gebǣran, *wv.(1b)*, [I-BERE]; be-
have, conduct oneself: *inf.* 38.
See **beran**.

bǣre, **bǣran**, see **beran**.

bærnan, *wv.(1b)*; BURN (*tr*), kindle,
consume: *inf.* 1116. See **byrnan**.

be, *prep.w.dat.*, [BY]; concerning,
about: 1068V.

†**beado-rinc**, *m.a-stem*, [RINK];
battle-warrior: *gp.* **-a** 1109.
See **rinc**, **gūð-rinc**. 1P.

†**bēag-gyfa**, *m.n-stem*, [BEE]; ring-
GIVER, *i.e.*, lord: *gs.* **-an** 1102. NP.

-bealo,   see   **morðor-bealo**,
sweord-bealo.

bearm, *m.a-stem*, [BARM]; bosom,
lap, embrace: *ns.* 1137; *as.* 1144.

bearn, *n.a-stem*, [BAIRN]; child,
son: *dp.* **-um** 1074; *ap.* 1088,
1141.

befæstan, *wv.(1b)*; FASTEN, en-
trust to, make safe, give over to:
inf. 1115.

befeallan, *v.(7),* [BEFALL]; fall, deprive: *pp. w.dat..instr.* **befeallen** deprived of 1126. See **feallan.**

begeat, see **begitan.**

bēgen, *adj.,* [BO]; BOTH: *gpm.* **bēga** 1124.

begitan, *v.(5),* [BEGET]; get, obtain, befall: *pret.3s.* **begeat** 1068, 1146.

belēac, see **belūcan.**

†**belēosan,** *v.(2),* [FORLESE]; LOSE, be deprived of: *pp.w.dat., instr.,* **beloren** deprived of 1073.

beloren, see **belēosan.**

belūcan, *v.(2),* [BELOUKE]; LOCK, close: *pret.3s.* **belēac** 1132.

†**bemurnan,** *v.(3);* MOURN, bewail: *pret.3s.* **bemearn** 1077.

-benc, see **medo-benc.**

benemnan, *wv.(1b),* [BENAME]; name, declare, stipulate: *pret.3s.* **benemde** 1097. See *PPs* 88.3.4, 88.43.3–4, 94.11.2, *HbM* 50 for similar phrases.

‡**ben-geat,** *n.a-stem;* wound-GATE, *i.e.,* gash: *np.* **-o** 1121. 1P.

bēodan, *v.(2),* *w.dat.;* BID, offer: *pret.3p.* **budon** 1085.

-beorn, see **sige-beorn.**

†**bēor-sele,** *m.i-stem,* [SALE]; BEER-hall, banquet-building: *ds.* 1094. 2P.

beran, *v.(4);* BEAR, carry: *inf.* **bæran** 20H; *pres.3p.* **berað** 5 (weapons understood as object); *opt.3s.* **bǣre** 20. See **forð-beran.**

berstan, *v.(3), w.dat.;* BURST (*intr.*), fail, break to pieces: *inf.* 30 (may be *tr.,* cp. *Rdl* 4.8); *pret.3p.* **burston** 1121.

betst, see **gōd.**

bewitian, *wv.(2),* observe, hold to: *pres.3p.* **-iað** 1135.

gebīdan, *v.(1),* [BIDE]; endure, experience, live through: *pret.3s.* **gebād** 25.

†**bill,** *n.ja-stem,* [BILL]; battle-axe, sword (usually the latter): *gp.* **-a** 1144.

-bite, see **lāð-bite.**

blāc, *adj.,* [BLAKE]: bright, shining, pale: *gpm.* **-ra** 34V. Hlt 2 intended substantive 'pale-ones'. See *****hrēaw-blāc.**

blǣd, *m.a-stem,* life, power, glory, prosperity, renown: *ns.* 1124.

blōd, *n.a-stem;* BLOOD: *ns.* 1121.

†**bord,** *n.a-stem,* [BOARD]; board, *i.e.,* shield: *ns.* 29.

brǣce, see **brecan.**

brecan, *v.(4);* BREAK, violate: *opt.3s.* **brǣce** 1100.

brōðor, *m.r-stem;* BROTHER: *dp.* **brōðrum** 1074.

-brūn, see **sealo-brūn.**

budon, see **bēodan.**

-būend, see **eorð-būend.**

burh, *f.monos.-stem.* [BOROUGH, BURGH]; fortress, castle, walled town: *ns.* **buruh** 36V. See **buruh-þelu, Finnsburh, hēa-burh, Hildeburh.**

burston, see **berstan.**

‡**buruh-þelu,** *f.ō-stem,* [BOROUGH, BURGH + THEAL]; fortress-floor: *ns.* 30. *þelu,* always compounded, literally means 'plank'. See also **burh, Finns-buruh, hēa-burh, Hildeburh.** NP.

byldan, *wv.(1b),* [BIELD]; encourage, cheer, exhort: *inf.* 1094.

byrnan, *v.(3);* BURN (*intr.*): *pres.3p.* **-að** 1, 4. See **bærnan.**

byrne, *f.n-stem,* [BURNE, BRYN]; corselet, mail-coat: *ns.* 44.

C

‡**celæs,** *adj.,* (meaning unknown): *nsn.* 29. Variants. **celced,** chalked, whitened. **Cēled,** cooled, chilled; cp. *Bwf* 3021–2, *gār* . . .

morgenceald, (spear . . . morning-
cold) with both literal (dewy,
icy) and figurative (deadly)
meaning. **Cellod,** or **cēlod,**
leather-covered, from Kentish
cyllod < *cyll,* leather bag or bot-
tle; or keel-shaped, < *cēol;* or
beaked, < *cele* (BTS 121, citing
Epinal Gloss 862 : *Neb vel scipes caeli*
[*cæle, celae*] *rostrum*); or vaulted <
Latin *celatus.* See **ceorl.**

celced, cēled, cellod, cēlod, see
celæs.

cempa, *m.n-stem,* [KEMP]; cham-
pion, warrior: *np.* **-an** 14.

cene, *adj.;* KEEN, bold, brave: *dsm.*
(*collective*) or *dpm.* **-um** 29.

ceorl, *m.a-stem,* [CHURL]; man: *gs.*
(*collective*) **ceorlæs** (= *ceorles*)
29V. See **celæs.**

clǣne, *adj.* : CLEAN, true: *nsn.* 29V.

cōm, see **cuman.**

†**corðer,** *n.a-stem,* troop, band: *ds.*
corðre 1153.

†**cringan, gecringan,** *v.(3),*
[CRANK, CRINGE]; fall (in battle),
yield, die: *pret.3s.* **gecrang** 31;
pret.3p. **crungon** 1113.

crungon, see **cringan.**

cuman, *v.(4)*: COME: *pret.3s.* **cōm**
1077, 1133.

cūð, *adj.,* [COUTH]; known, famous,
familiar: *nsm.* 25; *npf.* **-e** 1145.

cwæð, see **cweðan.**

cwēn, *f.i-stem;* QUEEN, king's wife,
lady: *ns.* 1153.

cweðan, *v.(5),* [QUETHE, QUOTH];
say, speak: *pret.3s.* **cweþ** 24,
cwæð 1067V. See **oncweðan.**

cyn, see **cynn.**

cyning, *m.a-stem;* KING: *ns.* 2, 1153.
See **eorð-cyning.**

cynn, *n.ja-stem;* KIN, family, people:
as. **cyn** 1093.

D

dagas, see **dæg.**

dagian, *wv.(2).* [DAW]; dawn;
pres.3s. **dagað** 3.

-dǣd, see **wēa-dǣd.**

dæg, *m.a-stem;* DAY: *ap.* **dagas** 41.
See **dōgor.**

dǣl, *m.i-stem;* part, share, a great
DEAL of: *as.* 1150.

†**dēor-mōd,** *adj.,* [DEAR + MOOD];
fierce-minded, bold, brave: *nsm.*
23. See **mōd, ōn-mōd.** 1P.

dēð, see **dōn.**

dōgor, *n.a-stem,* DAY: *gp.* **dōgra**
1090. See **dæg.**

dohtor, *f.r-stem;* DAUGHTER: *ns.*
1076.

dōm, *m.a-stem,* [DOOM]; judgment,
decree, justice: *ds.* **-e** 1098.

dōn, *anom.v.;* DO, act, put, cause:
inf. 1116; *pres.3s.* **dēð** 1134;
pres.3p. **dōð** 1134V; *pret.3s.* **dyde**
1144.

draca, *m.n-stem,* [DRAKE]; dragon:
ns. 3.

drīfan, *v.(1)*; DRIVE, impel: *inf.*
1130.

‡**driht-gesīð,** *m.a-stem,* [DRIGHT +
SITHE]; army- or noble-com-
panion, retainer, warrior: *gp.*
-a 42. In military context, BP.

drihtlīc, *adj.,* [DRIGHT]; noble,
lordly: *asn.* **-e** 1158; *npm.* **-e** 14.

duru, *f.u-stem;* DOOR: *ds.* **dura** 14;
as. **-u** 23; *dp.* **-um** 16, 20; *ap.* **-u**
42, **-a** 42V.

dyde, see **dōn.**

dynnan, *wv.(1a)*; make a DIN,
resound: *pret.3s.* **dynede** 30.

E

ēac, *adv.,* [EKE]; also: 45.

†**eafera,** *m.n-stem,* offspring, son,
child, heir, successor, (*pl.*) re-
tainers: *dip.* **-um** 1068; *ip.***-um**
1068V; *ap.* **-an** 1068V.

ealdor, *n.a-stem,* life: *gs.* **ealdres**
1067V.

eal-gylden, *adj.*; ALL-GOLDEN, gild-
ed: *nsn.* 1111. See **eall.** NP.

eall, *adj.*; ALL: *nsf.* **eal** 36; *asn.* **eal**
22, 1086, 1155; *gpm.* **ealra** 32;
apm. **ealle** 22V, 1080, 1122.
Adj., used adverbially, = in all
respects: *gpn.* **ealles** 1129V. *Adv.*
quite, entirely: **eal** 1129. See
eal-gylden, eal-swā.

eal-swā, *adv.*; ALSO, too: 41V.
See **eall.**

ēam, *m.a-stem,* [EME]; *maternal*
uncle: *ds.* **-e** 1117V.

eard *m.a-stem,* [ERD]; native land,
country, home: *as.* 1129.

earme, *adv.,* [ARM]; wretchedly,
miserably: 1117; according to
Wrn 206, *adj.* wretched, *nsf.*

earn, *m.a-stem,* [ERNE]; eagle: *ns.*
ærn, earn 34V.

ēastan, *adv.*; from the EAST: 3.

eaxl, *f.ō-stem,* [AXLE]; shoulder:
ds. or *as.* **-e** 1117.

ecg, *f.jō-stem*; (sword)-EDGE, sword,
blade: *ns.* 1106; *np.* **-e** 1145.

efne, *adv.*; EVEN. just: 1092.

eft, *adv.,* [EFT]; afterwards, again,
thereafter: 1065V, 1146.

ellen, *mn.a-stem,* [ELNE]; courage,
strength, zeal: *ds.* **elne** 1097,
1129V; *as.* 11. *Elne* in 1097 may
be an instrumental intensive,
meaning 'much' or 'very'. Kock
[1096] 109 = *adv.,* strongly; see
unflitme. Always neuter in
poetry.

ende, *m.ja-stem*; END: *ns.* 1067V.

ēodon, see **gān.**

eofer, *m.a-stem,* [EVER]; boar, boar-
image (on a helmet): *ns.* 1112.

eom, *anom.v.,* [BE]; *am: pres.1s.* 24;
pres.3s. **is** 24, 26. Wesan, *v.(5),*
be: *imp.p.* **wesað** 12; *pret.3s.*
wæs 28, 45, 1063, 1067V, 1075,

1103, 1107, 1109, 1110, 1124,
1136, 1151, 1159; *pret.3p.* **wǣron**
1145; *opt.3s.* **wǣre** 36, 44, 1105.

†**eorð-büend,** *m.nd-stem*; EARTH-
dweller, man, native: *gp.* **-ra** 32,
i.e., the Frisians. See *Jud* 226,
314 *landbüend-* (land-dweller).
NP.

eorð-cyning, *m.a-stem,* [EARTH +
KING]; earth-king, ruler of a
country or tribe: *gs.* **-es** 1155.
NP.

eoten, *m.a-stem,* [ETEN]; giant,
monster, (figurative) enemy: *gp.*
-a 1072, 1088, 1141; *dp.* **-um**
1145. See **Ēotan** for variants.

ēower, *poss.pron.*; YOUR: *apf.* **ēowre**
11.

†**ēð-gesȳne,** *adj.,* [EATH]; easily-
SEEN, apparent, visible: 1110.
NP.

F

-fāh, see **swat-fāh, wæl-fāg.**

-fæt, see **bān-fæt.**

fæger, *adj.*; FAIR, beautiful, plea-
sant: *nsm.* 1137.

fæla, see **fela.**

fǣr, *m.a-stem,* [FEAR]; sudden
attack, disaster: *ns.* 1068; *as.*
fēr 5V.

fæst, *adj.*; FAST, firm: *asf.* **-e** 1096.

†**fǣted,** *adj.,* gold-ornamented or
-plated: *gsn.* **fǣttan** 1093; *apm.*
fǣtte 5V. < *pp.* of *fǣtan,* 'adorn,
cram, load'.

fēa, *adj.*; FEW: *dp.* **fēaum** 1081. See
ān.

feallan, *v.(7)*; FALL, fail, die: *inf.*
1070; *pret.3s.* **fēol** 41.

fēaum, see **fēa.**

fela, *indeclinable adj., w.part.gen.,*
[FELE]; many, much: **fæla** 25, 33.

‡**feoh-gift,** *f.i-stem,* [FEE; GIFT];
treasure-giving: *dp.* **feoh-gyftum**
1089. NP.

feohtan, *v.(3)*: FIGHT: *pret.3p.*
fuhton 41.

gefeohtan, *v.(3)*; win by FIGHT-
ING (usually), (here) fight to a
finish: *inf.* 1083.

fēol, see **feallan.**

fēond, *m.nd-stem,* [FIEND]; enemy:
np. **fȳnd** 5V; *gp.* **fēonda** 1152.

feorh, *mn.ua-stem,* life, body: *as.*
19; *dp.* **fēorum** 1152. See **feorh-
genīōla.**

†**feorh-genīōla,** *m.n-stem,* [NITH];
life-enemy, mortal-foe: *np.?* **-an**
5V. 2P.

fēorum, see **feorh.**

fēr, see **fǣr.**

fēran, *wv.(1b),* [FERE]: FARE, go,
march: *pret.3p.* **-aō** 5V.

‡**ferhō-frec,** *adj.,* [FRECK]; life-
bold, deadly-daring, brave: *asm.*
-an 1146. Wms 102–3 suggests
gsm., referring to Hengest.
Ferhō- literally means 'mind,
spirit, life'; in compounds, it
carries connotations of 'deadly-,
mortal-, savage-'. *-frec* means
'-greedy, -daring, -eager, -dan-
gerous'. Cp. **ferhō-grim, frēcne.**
1P.

†**ferhō-grim,** *adj.*; life-GRIM,
deadly-fierce, savage: *npm.* **-me**
41V. For *ferhō-,* see **ferhō-frec.**
-grim means also '-dire, -bitter,
-painful'. Cp. *Whl* 5, *Jul* 141,
frēcne ond ferōgrim, both referring
to villains. 1P.

ferian, *wv.(2),* [FERRY]; carry,
bring: *pret.3p.* **feredon** 1154, 1158.

-ferō, see **Sige-ferō.**

fīf, *num.*; FIVE: *apm.* 41.

findan, *v.(3)*; FIND, meet with,
discover, obtain by search, re-
cover: *inf.* 1156.

†**flacor,** *adj.,* [FLACKER, FLICKER?];
flickering, flying, quickly moving:
nsm. **flacra** 34V; *apm.* **flacre** 5V,

both late forms. Cp. *Glc* 1144,
Chr 676.

flacra, flacre, see **flacor.**

‡**flān-boga,** *m.n-stem,* [FLANE];
arrow-BOW: *apm.* **-an.** 5V. Cp.
Bwf 1433, 1744. NP.

flēogan, *v.(2)*; FLY: *pres.3s.* **-eō** 3.

flet, *n.ja-stem,,* [FLAT]; (hall)-floor,
hence hall *(synecdoche)*: *as.* 1086.
Klb 172–3 suggests *flet* may be a
row of benches, see notes.

flyht, *m.i-stem*; FLIGHT, flying: *ds.*
-e 5V. On *flyhte* = on the wing.

folc, *n.a-stem*; FOLK, people, nation,
tribe, troop, army: *gs.* **-es** 9,
46, 1124.

folde, *f.n-stem,* [FOLD]; earth,
ground, soil, country, region: *gs.*
-an 1137; *as.* **-an** 5V.

folgian, *wv.(2),* *w.dat.*; FOLLOW,
pursue, accompany, serve:
opt.3p. **folgedon** 1102.

for, fore, *prep.w.dat.,* [FORE]; be-
fore, in front of, in the presence
of: 1064, 1120.

forgyldan, *v.(3)*, [FORYIELD]; pay
for, repay, requite: *inf.* 39. Cp.
gyldan.

forhabban, *wv.(3)*, [HAVE]; hold
in, restrain: *inf.* 1151. Cp.
habban.

forma, *adj.,* *supl.,* [FORME]; first:
dsm. **-an** 19.

forniman, *v.(4)*, [FORNIM]; take
away, destroy, kill, *pret.3s.* **for-
nam** 1080, 1123. *For-* is an inten-
sive prefix often with connota-
tions of destruction. Cp. **for-
swelgan.** See **ānyman, niman.**

forswelgan, *v.(3)*, [FORSWALLOW];
SWALLOW up, devour, destroy:
pret.3s. **forswealg** 1122. See
forniman.

forō, *adv.*; FORTH, forward, away:
5, 41V. *Forō gerimed* = all told,
counted up. See **forō-beran.**

forð-beran, *v.(4)*, [FORTHBEAR]; bring FORTH: *pres.3p.* **forð-berað** 5V. See **forð.** NP.

forðringan, *v.(3)*, [FORTHRING]; rescue, protect, defend, push out: *inf.* 1084. Other suggested meanings: displace (Klb 3 1084n), crush utterly (Brown [245] 182 f.). put down (Moore [1467] 208 f.), force away from one (Wms 41 ff., 166 ff.), expel (Mal 115; Hoops [894] 57 f.). See note.

forwyrnan, *wv.(1b)*, *w.dat.person, gen.thing*, [FORWARN]; refuse, repudiate, hinder, oppose, withhold: *pret.3s.* **forwyrnde** 1142. See Brd 301–13.

fram, *prep.w.dat.*; FROM: 34V.

frægn, see **frignan.**

-frec, see **ferhð-frec.**

frēcne, *adj.*, [FRECK]; daring, dangerous, savage: *dsf.* **-en** 1104, late spelling. See **ferhð-frec.**

fremman, *wv.(1a)*, [FREME]; perform, do, perpetrate, carry out, bring about: *inf.* 9.

frēolīc, *adj.*, [FREELY]; free, noble, glorious, beautiful, excellent: *asn.* 19.

frēond, *m.nd-stem*; FRIEND, relative: *dp.* **-um** 1126.

frignan, *v.(3)*, [FRAYNE]; ask, inquire: *pret.3s.* **frægn** 22, 46. See **gefrignan.**

gefrignan, *v.(3)*, [FRAYNE]; learn by inquiring, hear about: *pret.1s.* **gefrægn** 37. See **frignan.**

†**frioðu-wǣr,** *f.ō-stem*, [FRITH + WARE]; peace-treaty: *as.* **-e** 1096. See **wǣr.** NP.

fromlīce, *adv.*, boldly, strongly, quickly: 41V.

fugol, *m.a-stem*; FOWL, bird: *np.* **fugelas** 5.

fuhton, see **feohtan.**

fundian, *wv.(2)*, [FOUND]; strive, depart, hasten, aspire, desire, yearn to go: *pret.3s.* **fundode** 1137.

fūslīc, *adj.*, [FOUS]; ready, excellent: *apn.* **fūslicu** 5V. Cp. *Bwf* 232, 2618. *Fūs* = eager to start, ready, hastening, willing, brave, noble.

fȳnd, see **fēond.**

-fȳr, see **wæl-fȳr.**

fyrd, *f.i-stem*, [FERD]; army: *ns.* 5V. See **fyrd-searo.**

‡**fyrd-searo,** *n.wa-stem*, [FERD]; army-trappings, armour: *ap.* **-u** 5V. *-searo* connotes skilful, even cunning manufacture. See *Bwf* 232, 2618, *inwit-searo, searo-gimm.* NP.

fȳren, *adj.*, [FIREN]; afire: fiery: *nsf.* **fȳrenu** 36.

G

-gamen, see **heal-gamen.**

gān *anom.v.*; GO: *pret.3p.* **ēodon** 14.

gangan *v.(7)*, [GANG]; go, walk: *inf.* 43. See **gegangan.**

gegangan, *v.(7)*, [GANG]; go to a place, reach, happen: *pp.* **gegongen** 1067V.

†**gār,** *m.a-stem*, [GARE]; spear, dart: *ds.* **-e** 1075. See **Hrōð-gār, Gār-ulf.**

gǣst, *m.a-stem*: GHOST, spirit, demon: *gp.* **-a** 1123.

geæfned, see **æfnan.**

gēar, *n.a-stem*; YEAR: *ns.* 1134.

geard, *m.a-stem*; YARD, enclosure, court, dwelling, land: *dp.* **-um** 1138 (singular meaning); *ap.* **-as** 1134.

gearu, *adj.wa-stem*, [YARE]; ready, finished, equipped: *ns.* 1109.

gearwe, *adv.*, [YARE]; well, thoroughly, entirely, quickly, surely: 11V.

-geat, see **ben-geat.**

gebād, see -bīdan.

-gebind, see īs-gebind.

gebyrd, *fn.i-stem*, [BIRDE]; BIRTH, parentage, quality, fate (here): *as*. 1074. Cosijn [389] 18 suggests *on gebyrd* = 'in succession, one after another'.

gecrang, see -cringan.

gefrægn, see -frignan.

gegongen, see -gangan.

gehlyn, *n.ja-stem*, [LINN?]; sound, din: *ns*. 28. See hlynnan.

gehwylc, *pron.*, *w.part.gen.*, [IWHILLC]; EACH, every one: *isn.* -e 1090.

gemænden, see -mænan.

-gemōt, see torn-gemōt.

gemunde, see -munan.

genǣson, see -nesan.

genumon, see niman.

gēomor, *adj.*, [YOMER]: sad, troubled, miserable, mournful: *nsf.* gēomuru 1075. See gēomrian.

gēomrian, *wv.*(2), [YOMER]; be sad, mourn, lament, complain: *pret.3s.* gēomrode 1118. See gēomor.

gēomuru, see gēomor.

-geong, see heaþo-geong, heoro-geong.

gerīmed, see -rīman.

gerȳmdon. see -rȳman.

-gesīð, see driht-gesīð.

-gesteald, see in-gesteald.

-gestreon, see sinc-gestreon.

-gesȳne, see ēð-gesȳne.

getruwedon, see -truwian.

getugon, see -tēon.

geþearfod, see -þearfian.

geþinge, *n.ja-stem*, [THING]; agreement, meeting, fate, (*pl.*) terms: *ap*. geðinge 1085.

gewāt, see -wītan.

geweald, *mn.a-stem*, [WIELD, IWALD]; power, possession, control, protection: *as*. 11V, 1087.

gewiton, see -wītan.

gidd, *n.ja-stem*, [YED]; song, poem, tale, formal speech, saying, riddle: *ns*. gid 1065, gyd 1160; *dp*. giddum 1118. Generally applied to oral, traditional knowledge.

gif, *conj.*; IF (*w.indicative*), whether (*w.opt.*): gyf 1104, gif 1140.

gīfre, *adj.*, [YEVER]; greedy: *supl.-nsm*. gīfrost 1123.

-gimm, see searo-gimm.

gist, *m.i-stem*; GUEST, visitor, stranger: *ns*. 1138.

glēo-mann, *m.a-stem*, [GLEEMAN]; minstrel, singer: *gs*. -es 1160. NP.

gnornian, *wv.*(2), be sad, mourn, lament, grieve: *pret.3s.* gnornode 1117.

gōd, *adj.*; GOOD, pleasant, proficient, considerable: *gpm*. gōdra 33; *supl.nsm*. betst 1109; *supl.asn.* sēlest 1144. See sēl.

gold, *n.a-stem*; GOLD: *ns*. 1107V; *gs*. -es 1093. See gold-hladen, inge-gold.

‡gold-hladen, *adj.*, [LADE]; GOLD-adorned: *nsm*. 13. *-hladen* < *pp.* of *hladan* 'load, lay on'. NP.

‡gomen-wudu, *m.u-stem*; [GAME]; mirth-WOOD, *i.e.*, harp: *ns*. 1065. See heal-gamen. NP.

‡grǣg-hama, *adj.*, [HAME]; GREY-coated: *nsm.*(*substantive*) 6. NP.

grētan, *wv.*(*1b*); GREET, approach, attack, touch. play (music): *pp.* grēted 1065.

grimm, *adj.*, GRIM, savage, severe, bitter, painful, angry; *asm.* grimne 1148.

gripe, *m.i-stem*; GRIP, grasp, attack: *as*. 1148.

guldan, see gyldan.

‡gum-þegn, *m.a-stem*, [GOME + THANE]; man-retainer: *nsm*. 13V. Cf. *GfM* 83 *gumþegnum*. *Gum-* < †*guma*, 'man, lord, hero'. NP.

†**gūð.** *f.ō-stem*, fight, battle, war:
ns. 1123; *ds.* **-e** 31. See **gūð
-here**, **-hring**, **-rēc**, **-rinc**, and
-wudu.

gūð-here, *m.ja-stem*, [HERE]; battle-
army: *as.* 18V. See Boer [141]
144 ff., *Gen* 1967 ‡*gūðhergum*.
See **gūð, here-sceorp, Gūðere.**
1P.

*****gūð-hring,** *m.a-stem*; battle-RING:
ns. 1118V. Grn 1 and *Sprach-
schatz* 281 = clamour, dirge. Sdg
3 = spirals of flame and smoke.
See **gūð, hring.** 1P.

*****gūð-rēc,** *m.i-stem*, [REEK]; battle-
smoke: *ns.* **-rēc** and **-rēoc** 1118V.
See GtD 284, Grn 2, TrF,
Rieger [1708] 395. *Bwf* 3144
wud(u)rēc (wood-smoke). See **gūð.**
1P.

†**gūð-rinc,** *m.a-stem*, [RINK]; battle-
warrior, -hero, -man: *ns.* 1118.
See **gūð, rinc, beado-rinc.**
1P.

‡**gūð-wudu.** *m.u-stem*; battle-WOOD,
i.e., spear (or possibly shield, *cf.*
bord): *ns.* 6. See **gūð.** 1P.

gyd, see **gidd.**

gyf, see **gif.**

-gyfan, see **bēag-gyfa.**

-gyft, see **feoh-gyft.**

gyldan, *v.(3)*; YIELD, pay, repay,
render: *pret.3p.* **guldan** 40. Cp.
forgyldan.

-gylden, see **eal-gylden.**

gyllan, *v.(3)*; YELL, shout, cry out,
resound: *pres.3s.* **-eð** 6.

gyrdan, *wv.(1b)*; GIRD on, belt on,
encircle: *pret.3s.* **gyrde** 13.

†**gyrn-wracu,** *f.ō-stem*, [WRACK,
WRAKE]; injury-revenge: *ds.*
-wræce 1138. *Gyrn* = sorrow,
misfortune, affliction, injury.
1P.

gȳt, *adv.*; YET, still, besides, even,
hitherto: 18, 26, 1127, 1134.

H

habban, *wv.(3)*; HAVE, hold, keep,
look after, get: *imp.p.* **-að** 11.
See **forhabban.**

†**hafela,** *m.n-stem*, head: *np.* 1120.

hām, *m.a-stem*; HOME, estate,
dwelling, region, country: *ds.*
1147, 1156; *ap.* **-as** 1127.

-hama, see **grǣg-hama.**

hand, *f.u-stem*; HAND, power, pos-
session: *ds.* **-a** 29; *gs., gp.,* or *ap.*
-a 11V.

hātan, *v.(7)*, [HIGHT]; command,
order, cause (?): *pret.3s.* **hēt**
1114.

hægsteald, *adj.*, unmarried, inde-
pendent, military (of a young
man), young; *substantive npm.*
-as 40.

†**hæleð,** *m.þ-stem.* [HELETH]; man,
warrior, hero: *ns.* 23, 43, 1069;
np. 41V.

hē, *pron*; HE: *nsm.*19, 22, 24, 1079,
1082, 1093, 1098, 1130, 1138,
1140, 1141, 1142; *gsm.* **his** 13, 40,
44, 45, 1147; *dsm.* **him** 17, 43,
1067V, 1143; *asm.* **hine** 13, 46,
hyne 33; *nsf.* **hēo** 1078, 1079V;
gsf. **hire** 1115; *asn.* **hit** 1106,
hyt 21; *np.* **hīe** 11H, 19V, 1074,
1086, 1087, 1102, 1156, 1157,
hīg 41, 42, 1085; *gp.* **hira** 39V,
1102, 1124, **hyra** 15, 41, 47;
dp. **him** 1085, 1086, 1103, 1125;
ap. **hīe** 1068.

hēa-burh, *f.monos.-stem*, [BOROUGH,
BURGH]; HIGH-fortress, chief-city,
elevated-town: *as.* 1127. See
burh, buruh-þelu. NP.

hēah-setl, *n.a-stem*, [SETTLE]; HIGH-
seat, *i.e.*, throne: *as.* 1087. NP.

healdan, *v.(7)*; HOLD, guard, oc-
cupy, possess, regard, rule, treat:
*pret. 3s.***hēold** 1079; *pret.3p.***hēold-
on** 42; *opt.3s.* **hēolde** 23, 1099.

healf, *f.ō-stem;* HALF, side, part:
ap. **-a** 1095.

healf, *adj.;* HALF; *gsf.* **-re** 1087;
asn. **-ne** 1087V.

‡**heal-gamen,** *n.a-stem;* HALL-
GAME, entertainment: *as.* 1066.
See **heall, gomen-wudu.** NP.

heall, *f.ō-stem;* HALL, dwelling,
palace, (here) mead-hall; *ns.*
heal 1151; *gs.* **-e** 4, 20; *ds.* **-e** 28;
-e 1087. See **heal-gamen.**

hēap, *m.a-stem,* [HEAP]; multitude,
throng, troop: *as.* 1091.

heard, *adj.;* HARD, severe, cruel,
violent, strong, bold: *substantive
ns.* 21 (= Sigeferð); *gp.* **heardra**
26V, **heordra** 26. See **īren-
heard.**

‡**hearo-geong,** *adj.;* sword-YOUNG,
battle-young: *nsm.* 2. Means 'less
experienced in warfare than one
would expect of a *cyning'.* Alter-.
nate spelling **heoro-geong** 2V.
See **heaðo-geong, heaðo-georn.**
1P.

*heaðo-geong,** *adj.;* war-YOUNG,
young in battle: *nsm.* 2V. Ap-
proximately the same as **hearo-
geong,** *q.v.* See also **heaðo-
georn.** *Heaðo-* appears only in
compounds. NP.

*heaðo-georn,** *adj.,* [YEARN]; war-
eager: *nsm.* 2V. See **heaðo-
geong, hearo-geong.** NP.

hebban, *v.(6);* HEAVE, raise up,
lift: *imp.3p.* **hebbað** 11V.

helm, *m.a-stem,* [HELM]; protec-
tion, cover, (†)lord, helmet: *ns.*
45. See **bān-helm.**

hēo, see **hē.**

hēold, hēolde, hēoldon, see **heald-
an.**

heordra, see **heard.**

heoro-geong, see **hearo-geong.**

hēr, *adv.;* HERE, hither: 3, 4, 5, 5V,
26.

‡**here-sceorp,** *n.a-stem,* [HERE];
army-clothing, battle-equipment,
i.e., armour: *ns.* 45V; *dp.* **-um** 45.
See **gūð-here.** NP.

herian, *wv.(1a).* [HERY]; praise,
honour, command: *inf.* 1071.

hēt, see **hātan.**

-hete, see **morðor-hete.**

hicgeað, see **hycgan.**

hīegeað, see **hīgian.**

hīgian, *wv.(2),* [HIE]; strive, has-
ten: *imp.p.* **hīegeað** 11V. See
hycgan.

†**hild,** *f.jō-stem,* war, battle, combat:
ds. **-e** 37; *gp.* **-a** 26. See **hilde-
lēoma, hilde-wīsa, hild-plega.**

‡**hilde-lēoma,** *m.n-stem,* [LEAM];
battle-light (here a kenning for
sword): *as.* **hilde-lēoman** 1143.
See *Bwf* 1523 *beado-lēoma* (battle-
light) and 2583 *hilde-lēoman* (pro-
bably dragon flames and sword
flashes). See **hild, sweord-
lēoma.** 1P.

‡**hilde-wīsa,** *m.n-stem,* [WISE?];
battle-leader, commander: *ds.*
(or *dp.?*) **-an** 1064. See **hild.** BP.

‡**hild-plega,** *m.n-stem;* battle-PLAY,
war-sport: *ds.* 1073MS. See **hild,
lind-plega.** 1P.

him, hine, hira, hire, his, hit, see
hē.

*hlacor,** *adj.,* screaming: *nsm.*
hlacra 34V. See Holthausen
[862] 256 and Hlt 7: ? < *hla-
cerian,* 'to mock, deride'.

-hladen, see **gold-hladen.**

†**hlāw,** *mn.a-stem,* [LOW]; mound,
cairn, cave, barrow, burial-
mound: *ds.* **-e** 1120. See Cmb
636.

‡**hlence,** *f.n-stem,* link, coat of
mail: *ap.* **hlencan** 11V. See
Exo 218 *hlencan, Exo* 176, *Ele*
24 *wæl-hlencan* (slaughter-mail),
and O. Cockayne, *Leechdoms,*

‡**hlence**—*contd.*
  Wortcunning and Starcraft of Early England (London, 1864–6), II, 342, 4 *gehlenced* (iron-bound).

hlēoðrian, *wv.*(2), speak, cry aloud, exclaim, sing, resound: *pret.3s.* **hlēoðrode** 2.

hlynnan, *wv.*(*1a*), [LINN?]; make noise, shout, roar, resound: *pres.3s.* **hlynneð** 6; *pret.3s.* **hlynode** 1120. See **gehlyn.**

hōlinga, *adv.*, in vain, without reason or cause: 1076.

holm, *m.a-stem,* [HOLM]; (†) wave, sea, ocean, water: *ns.* 1131. See Wyld [2270] 55 and Metzenthin, *JEGP,* 21 (1922), 480–6.

hord, *mn.a-stem:* HOARD, something hidden, treasure, treasury: *ds.* **-e** 1108.

horn, *m.a-stem;* HORN, projection, pinnacle, gable: *ap.* **-as** 1, 4. See Miller [1450] and Cramp [402] 73.

hræfen, see **hrefn.**

hræs, see **hrēosan.**

hrǣw, *mn.a-stem,* [RAW?]; body, corpse, carrion: *ns., as., np., ap.* 34V. See **hrēaw-blāc.**

hrēas, see **hrēosan.**

*****hrēaw-blāc,** *adj.,* [RAW? + BLAKE]; corpse-pale: *substantive gpm.* **-ra** 34V. TrF '*totenbleichen*'; *hrēaw* = *hrǣw, q.v.* See **blāc,** NP.

hrefn, *m.a-stem;* RAVEN: *ns.* **hræfen** 34.

*****hrēodan,** *v.*(2), adorn, decorate: *pp.* **hroden** 1151. Used here figuratively and with grim irony; see **rēodan.**

hrēosan, *v.*(2), [REOSE]; fall, sink, RUSH, attack: *pret.3s.* **hrǣs, hrēas** 34V; *pret.3p.* **hruron** 1074. Connotations of death. See **āhrēosan.**

†**hreðer.** *m.a-stem,* breast, heart, mind, thought: *ds.* **hreðre** 1151.

hring, *m.a-stem;* RING, link, any circular thing, spiral, (gold) circlet: *dp.* **-um** 1091. See **hringed-stefna, gūð-hring.**

‡**hringed-stefna;** *m.n-stem,* RING-STEM, ring-prowed-ship, *as.* **-an** 1131. May refer to a ring-shaped, spiral, or simply curved stem; *cf.* the Oseberg ship. Various compounds in *Bwf* seem to describe this or similar prows: ‡*bundenstefna* 'bound-prow' 1910, ‡*wunden-stefna* 'wound-prow' 220, ‡*hringed-stefna* 32, 1897, ‡*hringnaca* 'ring-ship' 1862. See Falk [557] 38; Heyne [817] 42 and n. 3; Neckel [1550] 15, n. 2; K. Weinhold, *Altnordisches Leben* (*Berlin,* 1856), 483; and Snorri Sturluson's *Prose Edda* XLIX: Baldr's ship 'Hring-horni'. IP.

hroden, See **hrēodan.**

hrōr, *adj.,* [ROAR?]; active, vigorous, strong, brave: *nsm.* (modifying *hæleð* 43a) or *nsf.* (modifying *byrne?*) 45. See **unhrōr.**

hruron, see **hrēosan.**

hryre, *m.i-stem,* [RURE]; fall, ruin, destruction: *ns.*34V. < *hrēosan, q.v.*

hū, *adv.;* HOW: 47.

hungrig, *adj.;* HUNGRY: *nsm.* 34V.

hūru, *adv.,* [HURE]; indeed, at any rate, especially: 1071.

hwā, *pron.;* WHO: 23.

hwǣr, *conj.;* WHERE: 34.

hwæðer, *conj.* or *pron.;* WHETHER (*conj.*) or which of two (*pron.*): 48.

hwearf, see **hweorfan.**

hwearflic, *adj.,* [WHARVE?]; changing, transitory: *substantive gp.* **-ra** 34. Klb 252: 'active, agile, obedient, trusty'; Mak 266: 'mortal, dead, fleeting', comparing Alfred's Boethius (ed. W. J. Sedgefield, Oxford, 1899) 25.10; *hwerflic.* Klb 252 cites ON.

hverfr 'shifting'; *Lindisfarne Gospel* gloss *huoerflice* = *vicissim*; and *GfM* 68 *þegn gehweorf* (active? retainer).

hweorfan, *v.(3),* [WHARVE]; turn, go, roam, depart, return, die, convert: *pret.3s.* 17, 34V.

hwīt, *adj.*; WHITE, shining, bright, glistening, flashing, clear, fair, pale or dull yellow, golden: *asm.* **-ne** 39.

hwylc, *adj., w.part.gen.,* [WHICH]; any one: *nsm.* 1104.

hycgan, *wv.(3),* [HOW]; think, resolve, remember: *imp.p.* **hicgeaðð** 11, **hycgeaðð** 11V. Cp. *Exo* 218 *hycgan on ellen* 'think about courage'.

hyne, hyra, see **hē.**

hyrde, *m.ja-stem,* [HERD]: herder, shepherd, guardian, keeper, leader: *ns.* 46.

†**hyrst,** *f.i-stem,* ornament, jewel, treasure, trappings, armour: *ap.* **-a** 20.

†**hyse,** *m.i-stem,* youth, son, young warrior: *gp.* **hyssa** 48.

hyt, see **hē.**

I

ic, *pron.*; I: *ns.* 24, 25, 37; *ds.* **mē** 27; *dp.* **ūs** 5V.

‡**icge,** *adj.,* (meaning unknown): *nsn.* 1107MS. Brett [212] 2 suggests 'mighty', and others suggest 'treasure, rich, costly, massive'. Bouman [175] 143 f. < Kentish *ecge* 'by (on) the spearpoint'. Klaeber [1058] 256 < *æce* 'one's own (?)' on Isle of Wight sword. Most editors emend; see **æðeling, andīege, īdge, inge-gold, ītig, ondīege, ondlicge.** Cp. *Bwf* 2577 *incge-lāfe,* equally obscure, but see **inge-gold.**

ides, *f.i-stem,* (†) woman, lady, queen, wife: *ns.* 1075, 1117.

‡**idge,** *adv.*(?), eagerly?: 1107V. See Holthausen [855] 324–5 and Hlt 3–5, citing *Phx* 407 *idge* < **idig* busy?, active?'. Holthausen [865] 364 = *adj.* resplendent. See **icge** and **inge-gold.**

in, *prep., w.dat. of rest. acc. of motion*; IN, into: 1070, 1134, 1151.

*inge-gold, *n.a-stem*; native-GOLD, *i.e.,* gold from Finn's national or personal treasury: *ns.* 1107. See Rosier [1734] for this interpretation: cp. **icge** and *Bwf* 2577 *incge-lāfe* > **inge-lafe* 'native-remnant', again Rosier's emendation. See **ingesteald.** NP.

‡**ingesteald,** *n.a-stem*; native-property, house-property, goods of the household: *as.* 1155. See Rosier [1734]. 2P?.

inne, *adv.*; IN, inside, therein: 1141.

‡**inwit-searo,** *n.wa-stem,* malicious-skill, hostile-plot, enmity: *as.* 1101. *Inwit-* = evil, deceit, wicked, hostile, spiteful, treacherous, unfriendly, cunning, crafty; *-searo* = art, skill, cunning, trick, ambush, plot, treachery, armour. Both elements may carry connotations of malice and treachery. See **searo-gim, fyrd-searo.** NP.

īren, *n.ja-stem*; IRON, (†)iron-weapon, (†)sword: *ds.* **irne** 1141V. See **iren-heard.**

‡**īren-heard,** *adj.*; IRON + HARD: *npm.* 1112. See **īren.** NP.

irne, see **īren.**

is, see **eom.**

‡ **īs-gebind,** *n.a-stem,* [BIND]; ICE-bond, ice-fetter: *ds.* **-e** 1133. NP.

*ītig, *adj.,* splendid (?): *nsn.* ***itge** 1107V. Hlt 1–2 follows Hollander [836], who cites ON. *itr* 'glorious, excellent'. See **icge.**

L

lāc, *n.a-stem* or *f.ō-stem*, [LAKE]; play, battle, fight, gift, medicine, sacrifice: *gp*. **lācra** 5V. See Osborn 186–7.

-lād, see **sǣ-lād**.

-lāf, see **Gūðlāf, Hūnlāfing, Ordlāf, Ōslāf, wēa-lāf**.

land, *n.a-stem*; LAND, earth, territory, country (not-urban), realm: *as*. 11V; *gp*. **-a** 11H. See **Frȳsland**.

lāst, *m.a-stem*, [LAST]; foot-sole, footprint, track, step: *is*. **-e** 17. *On lāste* = behind, after.

lāð, *adj*., [LOATH]; hostile, hateful, evil, unpleasant: *substantive gpm*. 34V. See **lāð-bite**.

‡**lāð-bite**, *m.i-stem*, [LOATH]; hostile-BITE, *i.e.*, wound: *np*. or *ds*. 1122. See DbB 176. NP.

lǣdan, *wv.*(1*b*); LEAD, bring, conduct, take: *pret.3p*. **lǣddon** 1159.

lēod, *m.i-stem*, [LEDE]; man, (†) prince or king; (*pl*.) people, nation: *ns*. 24; *dp*. **-um** 1159.

lēof, *adj*., [LIEF]; beloved, dear, pleasant: *substantive dp*. **-um** 1073.

-lēoma, see **hilde-lēoma, sweord-lēoma**.

lēoð, *n.a-stem*, [LEOTH]; song, lay, poem: *ns*. 1159.

līc, *n.a-stem*. [LICH]; (living)-body, corpse: *gs*. **-es** 1122.

līg, *m.i-stem*, [LEYE]; flame, fire: *ns*. 1122.

lind, *f.jō-stem*, [LIND]; linden, (†) lindenwood-shield: *ap*. **-a** 11. See **lind-plega**.

‡**lind-plega**, *m.n-stem*, [LIND]; lindenshield-PLAY, battle: *ds*. **-plegan** 1073. *Plega < plegan*, 'to move quickly'. See **lind, hild-plega**, and *Bwf* 2039. NP.

M

māga, see **mǣg**.

magan, *prp.v.*(5); MAY, might, can, could, be strong, prevail: *pret.3s*. **meahte** 1078, 1130, 1150, **mehte** 1082; *pret.3p*. **meahton** 1156; *opt.3s*. **mihte** 1140.

manig, see **monig**.

mann, *m.a-stem*; MAN: *ns*. 1099. See **glēo-mann**.

mǣg, *m.a-stem*, [MAY]; male kinsman, compatriot: *gp*. **māga** 1079.

mǣnan, *wv.*(1*b*), [MEAN]; speak about, complain, lament, sorrow; *inf*. 1067; *pret. 3p*. **mǣndon** 1149. See **gemǣnan**.

gemǣnan, *wv.*(1*b*), [MEAN]; mention, complain: *pret.opt.3p*. **gemǣnden** 1101.

mǣnig, see **monig**.

mǣst, see **micel**.

mē. see **ic**.

meahte, meahton, see **magan**.

medo, *m.u-stem*; MEAD: *as*. 39, 39V. See **medo-benc, medo-drinc**.

†**medo-benc**, *f.i-stem*; MEAD-BENCH, *i.e.*, hall-seat: *ds*. **-e** 1067. See **medo, medo-drinc**. NP.

‡**medo-drinc**, *m.a-stem*; MEAD-DRINK: *as*. 39V. Cp. *Sfr* 22 *medodrince*. See **medo, medo-benc**. NP.

mehte, see **magan**.

meltan, *v.*(3); MELT, burn up, dissolve: *pret.3p*. **multon** 1120.

meotod-sceaft, see **metod-sceaft**.

mere, *m.i-stem*; MERE, pool, lake, (†)sea: *as*. 1130.

†**metod-sceaft**, *f.i-stem*, [METE? + SHAFT?]; fate-decree, doom, death: *as*. **meotod-sceaft** 1077. 1P.

†**meðel-stede**, *m.i-stem*. [MELL, MATHELE + STEAD]: speaking-

place, assembly-place, battle-field: *ds.* 1082. NP.

micel, *adj.,* [MICKLE]; much, great. large, many: *supl.nsn.* **mǣst** 1119; *asf.* **mǣste** 1079.

mid, *prep., w.dat.,* [MID]; with, among, together with: 1128, 1145.

mihte, see **magan.**

mīn, *poss.pron.;* MY, MINE: **mīne** 10, 13V; 24.

mōd, *n.a-stem,* [MOOD]; mind, heart, spirit, courage, pride, violence, power: *ns.* 1150. See **dēor-mōd, ōn-mōd.**

mōna, *m.n-stem;* MOON: *ns.* 7.

monig, *adj.:* MANY, many a: *nsm.* **mænig** 13, **manig** 1112.

morgen, *m.ja-stem;* MORN, morning, sunrise: *ns.* 1077.

‡**morðor-bealo,** *n.wa-stem;* MURDER + BALE, slaughter: *as.* 1079. *Bealo* = injury, destruction, evil, wickness, malice. 2P.

‡**morðor-hete,** *m.i-stem:* MURDER + HATE, murderous-hostility: *gs.* **-es** 1105. *Hete* = envy, malice, hostility, persecution, punishment. NP.

multon, see **meltan.**

mōtan, *prp.v.(6),* [MOTE]; may, must, be allowed to, have an opportunity to: *opt.3p.* **mōston** 1088.

multon, see **meltan.**

gemunan, *prp.v.(4), w.acc.,* [I-MUNE]; remember, be mindful of, think about, consider, mention: *pret.3s.* **gemunde** 1129; *opt.3s.* **gemunde** 1141.

myndgian, *wv.(2),* [MING]; remind, remember, mention, exhort: *pres.ptc.* **myndgiend** 1105.

N

nacod, *adj.;* NAKED, bare: *dpn.* **-um** 39V.

nalæs, nalles, see **nealles.**

nama, *m.n-stem;* NAME, reputation: *ns.* 24.

nān, *pron., adj.;* no, (*w.part.gen.*) NONE: 41.

nǣfre, *adv.;* NEVER: 1,37, **nēfre** 39.

nǣglian, *wv.(1);* NAIL, fasten with nails: *pp.nsn.* **nǣglod** 29V. See **celæs.**

ne, *adv.,* [NE]; not: 3, 4, 20, 37, 41, 1071, 1082, 1100, 1130, 1142, 1150.

nē, *conj.,* [NE]; nor; 3, 4, 39, 39V, 1084, 1100, 1101.

nealles, *adv.;* NOT at ALL, **nalles** 5V, 1076, **nalæs** 29V.

nēfre, see **nǣfre.**

nemne, *prep., w.dat.,* except: 1081.

nēosian, *wv.(2), w.gen.,* seek out, visit, go to, attack: *inf.* 1125.

genesan, *v.(5),* escape, survive, get through safely, bear: *pret.3p.* **genǣson** 47.

nigon, *num.;* NINE: *apm.* 41V.

niht, *f.monos-stem;* NIGHT, darkness, 24 hours: *gp.* **-a** 41V; *ap.* 41 V.

niman, *v.(4),* [NIM]; take, seize, grasp, carry off: *pp.* **numen** 1153. See **ānyman, forniman.**

nīð, *m.a-stem,* [NITH]; strife, enmity, attack, war, evil, hatred, affliction, grief, hostility, hostile-acts, (†)battle: *as.* 9; *gp.* **niða** 21.

nū, *conj., adv.;* NOW, now that, since: 7, 8, 10, 21, 39V, 1134.

numen, see **niman.**

O

of, *prep., w.dat.;* OF, from, out of, among, concerning, by, belonging to: 13V, 1108, 1138.

ofer, *prep., w.dat. of rest, acc. of motion;* OVER, above, across, in, against, beyond, after: 5V, 22, 1064V.

oft, *adv.,* [OFT]; often: 1065.

on, *prep.w.dat.*, *acc.*; ON, in, at, among, to, about, into, toward, against: 5V, 11, 12, 17, 28, 29, 43, 1074, 1082, 1094, 1095, 1109, 1113, 1116, 1117, 1130, 1144, 1153, 1157.

oncweðan, *v.(5),* [QUOTH, QUETHE]; answer, respond, echo, protest: *pret.3s.* **oncwyð** 7. See **cweðan.**

ond, see **and.**

*ondiege, *adv.*, openly (?): 1107V. < Gothic *andaugjo.* 'openly'. See Bgg 30, and **andiege.**

*ondlicge, *adj.*, lying stored (?): *nsn.* 1107V. See Sdg 3, *s.v. andlicge.*

ōn-mōd, *adj.*, [MOOD, ANMOD]; 'ONE-minded', steadfast, resolute, eager, bold, brave, fierce, proud: *npm.* **-e** 12. Cp. *Bwf* 2667 *an-hȳdig,* 'resolute'. See **mōd, dēor-mōd.** NP.

onwacnian, *wv.(2),* AWAKE, wake up *(intr.),* arise, spring up: *imp.p.* **onwæcnigeað** 10, **onwæcnað** 10V.

onweg, *adv.*; AWAY, forth, out, off, onward, along: 43V.

ord, *m.a-stem,* [ORD]; point, spear-point, spear, beginning, front, vanguard, prince: *ds.* **-e** 12.

oð, *conj.*, until: 31.

ōðer, *adj.*; OTHER, one of two, another, following: *nsn.* 1133: *asn.* 41V, 1086; *dpf.* **ōðrum** 16; *dpm.* **ōðrum** 34V.

oððæt, *conj.*, until, 1133. Often written as two words.

oððe, *conj.*, [OTHER]; or: 48.

P

-plega, see **hild-plega, lind-plega.**

R

†**rand,** *m.a-stem,* [RAND]; shield-boss or -border, shield, *ap.* **-as** 11V. See **rond-wīgend.**

-rædenne, see **worold-ræden.**

ræst, *f.jō-stem*; REST, resting-place, bed, grave: *ds.* **ræste, reste** 13V.

rēodan, *v.(2),* [RED, REOD]; redden, stain with blood: *pp.* **roden** 1151V. See ***hrēodan.**

reste, see **ræst.**

rīman, *wv.(1b),* [RIME]; count, number, reckon, tell, esteem as: *pp.* **gerīmed** 41V.

†**rinc,** *m.a-stem,* [RINK]; man, warrior, hero: *np.* **-as** 5V, 13V. See **beado-rinc, gūð-rinc.**

-rinc, see **gūð-rinc.**

roden, see **rēodan.**

†**rond-wīgend,** *m.nd-stem,* [RAND + WYE]; shield-fighter, warrior: *ns.* 13V. See **rand, wīgend.** BP.

rūm-heort, *adj.*; ROOMY-HEART, 'big-hearted', generous, carefree, noble-spirited: *substantive nsm.* 13V. NP.

gerȳman, *wv.(1b),* [RIME]; make roomy, enlarge, clear, vacate, widen, retire, yield: *pret.opt.3p.* **gerȳmdon** 1086.

S

samod, *adv.*, [SAMED]; also, together: 1063.

sang, *m.a-stem*; SONG, singing, noise, poem, lay: *ns.* 1063; *as.* 39V. See **singan.**

sæde, see **secgan.**

sæl, *mf.i-stem,* [SELE]; time, proper time, opportunity, occasion: *ap.* **sēle** 1135.

†**sæ-lād,** *f.ō-stem,* [LODE]; SEA journey, -path, -way, voyage: *ds.* **-e** 1139, 1157. See **sæ-sīð** NP.

‡**sæ-sīð,** *m.a-stem,* [SITHE]; SEA-journey, -expedition, -way, voyage: *ds.* **-e** 1149. See **sæ-lād.** NP.

scacan, *v.(6),* [SHAKE]: hasten, pass,

depart, shake, go, proceed, flee, move quickly to and fro: *pp.*
scacen 1124, 1136. See Wyld [2270] 85 ff.
sceft, *m.a-stem*; SHAFT, *synecdoche for* arrow *or* spear: *ds.* **-e** 7.
sceolde, see **sculan.**
-sceorp, see **here-sceorp.**
†**scēotend,** *m.nd-stem,* [SHOOT]; shooter, bowman, warrior: *np.* 1154. < *scēotan,* 'shoot'.
scildas, see **scyld.**
scīnan, *v.(1)*; SHINE, flash, be resplendent: *pres.3s.* **scȳneð** 7.
scip, *n.a-stem*; SHIP: *dp.* **scypon** 1154.
scolde, see **sculan.**
scop, *m.a-stem,* [SCOP]; poet, singer: *ns.* 1066.
sculan, *prp.v.(4)*; SHALL, must, ought to, be obliged to: *pret.3s.* **sceolde** 29, **scolde** 1067, 1070, 1106.
scyld, *m.a-stem,* *(originally u-stem)*; SHIELD: *ns.* 7; *ap.* **-as** 5V.
scȳneð, see **scīnan.**
scypon, see **scip.**
scȳran, *wv.(1b),* [SHIRE]; make clear, declare, arrange, decide, decree, settle: *inf.* 1106V. DbB 174 rejects on alliterative grounds.
sē, *dem.pron., adj., and art.*; THE, THAT, it, who, which, what: *nsm.* 1068; *nsf.* **sēo** 1153; *gsm.* **þæs** 1105; *gsm. or gsn.?* **þæs** 1145; *gsf.* **þǣre** 20; *dsm.* **þǣm** 1082, 1110, **þām** 1073; *dsf.* **þǣre** 31; *asf.* **þā** 23, 1084, 1098; *npm.* **þā** 47, 1125, 1135; *gpm.* **þǣra** 48; *gpn.?* **þāra** 1123; *dpn.?* **þām** 1135V; *apf.* **þā** 42.
‡**sealo-brūn,** *adj.,* [SALLOW + BROWN]; sallow-, dusky-, dark-brown: *nsm.* 35. Both elements = dark, dusky; *brūn* also means 'shining, having metallic lustre'. NP.

-searo, see **fyrd-searo, inwit-searo.**
searo-gim, *m.a-stem*; artistic-GEM, precious jewel: *gp.* **-rua** 1157. See **fyrd-searo, inwit-searo.** NP.
sēcean, *wv.(1c)*; SEEK, search for, try to get, desire, inquire, try, visit, approach, attack, proceed: *inf.* 27.
secgan, *wv.(3)*: SAY, tell, explain: *pret.3s.* **sǣde** 44.
sehtan, *wv.(1a),* [SAUGHT]; settle, adjust: *inf.* 1106V. See Sdg 1–2 and Brown [246] 912. DbB 174 objects to *sehtan* as probably a later Scandinavian loanword, citing E. Björkman, *Scandinavian Loan-Words in Middle English* (Halle, 1900), I, 100. See **sēman.**
sēl, *adv.,* [SELE]; better: 38, 39. See **gōd.**
sēle, see **sǣl.**
-sele, see **bēor-sele.**
sēlest, see **gōd.**
self, *pron.*; SELF, (his) own; *nsm.* **sylf** 17, 27; *gsm.* **selfes** 1147; *gsf.* **selfre** 1115.
sēman, *wv.(1b),* [SEEM]; settle, adjust: *inf.* 1106V. See **sehtan.**
sēo, see **sē.**
gesēon, *v.(5)* (I-SEE]; SEE, perceive, know, inspect, visit: *inf.* 1078, 1126.
-setl, see **hēah-setl.**
sēðan, *wv.(1b),* [SOOTH]; declare, affirm, testify, prove, decide (?), settle (?): *inf.* 1106V. See Klaeber [1058] 255 f. < *sōð* 'truth'.
sidian, *wv.(2),* arrange, set right, order: *inf.* 1106V. See Holthausen [887] 164.
‡**sige-beorn,** *m.a-stem,* [SIȝE + BERNE]; victory-man, -warrior, -noble, -hero, -prince: *gp.* **-a** 38. 2P.

r*

sige-drihten, *m.a-stem*, [SIჳE + DRIGHTIN]: victory-ruler, -king, -lord, -prince: *ds.* **sige-dryhtne** 39V. NP.

sigle, *n.ja-stem*, necklace, brooch, collar, jewel: *gp.* **-a** 1157.

†**sinc-gestrēon,** *n.a-stem*, [STRAIN]; treasure-wealth: *dp.* **-um** 1092. *Sinc* = treasure, valuables, gold, jewel; *gestrēon* = gain, acquisition, property, treasure, wealth. 1P.

singāla, *adv.* continually, always: **syngāles** 1135.

singan, *v.(3)*; SING, ring out, chant, narrate, resound, ring, clank: *pres.3p.* **singað** 5. See **āsingan.**

sīð, *m.a-stem*, [SITHE]; going, journey, voyage, adventure, expedition, fate, way, time, occasion, advance, rush: *ds.* **sīðe** 19. See **sǣ-sīð.**

sīððan, *adv.,* [SITHEN]; afterwards, thereafter: 1106; *conj.,* since, when, after, because(?): 1077, 1148.

sixtig, *num.*; SIXTY: *ap.* 38.

slēan, *v.(6)*; SLAY, strike, rush; *pp.* **slægen** 1152.

-slihta, see **wæl-sliht.**

slīðen, *adj.,* cruel, hard, evil, dire: *nsn.* 1147.

sōna, *adv.*; SOON, immediately, at once: 46.

sorh, *f.ō-stem*; SORROW, pain, grief, trouble, anxiety: *as.* **sorge** 1149.

sprǣc, *f.jō-stem*; SPEECH, language, statement, narrative, conversation, rumour, charge, question: *ds.* **-e** 1104.

standan, *v.(6)*; STAND, continue, stay firm, exist, happen, oppose, stop; (†)appear, flash: *imp.p.* **standað** 12V; *pret.3s.* **stōd** 35. **-stede,** see **meðel-stede.**

-stefna, see **hringed-stefna.**

stēoran, *wv.(1b)*, *w.dat.*; STEER, direct, rule, correct, (*here*) restrain: *pret.3s.* **stȳrde** 18V.

stōd, see **standan.**

storm, *m.a-stem*; STORM; (†, *figurative?*) rush, attack, disturbance: *ds.* **-e** 1131.

stȳrde, see **stēoran.**

styrian, *wv.(1b)*; STIR up, disturb, incite, excite, exhort, rouse, cause, tell; *pret.3s.* **styrede** 18V, **styrode** 18. *Styrode* LWS; see Cmb 749.

sum, *adj.*; SOME, a certain: *npm.* **-e** 1113. Litotes, meaning here 'many'.

sunu, *m.u-stem*; SON, descendant: *ns.* 33, 1089; *as.* 1115.

swā, *adv.*; SO, thus, in this manner: 19, 39H, 1103, 1142; *conj.,* as: 41, 1092, 1093, 1134. See Brd 286–301.

swān, *m.a-stem* [SWAIN, SWON]; herdsman; (†)young man, warrior?: *ap.* **-as** 39. See note.

†**swāt-fāh,** *adj.,* [SWEAT + FAW]; blood-stained, bloody: *nsf.* 1111. *Fāh* = 'variegated, spotted, dappled, coloured, stained, dyed, shining, gleaming', *as well as* 'hostile, proscribed, outlawed, guilty, criminal'. See **wæl-fāg.** NP.

swæðer, *pron.,* [SO, WHETHER]; whichever of two: *asn.* 27. = *swā* + *hwæðer*, *qqv.*; cp. *Bwf* 686 *on swa hwæþere hond* (on which of two sides).

sweart, *adj.,* [SWART]; swarthy, black, dark, gloomy, evil, infamous: *nsm.* 35.

swēg, *m.i-stem*, [SWEY?]; sound, noise, melody, voice: *ns.* 1063. < *swōgan*, 'sound, roar, howl, whistle, rattle, rustle'.

†**swegl**, *n.a-stem*, sky, heaven, sun: *ds.* **-e** 1078.

sweoloð, *mn.a-stem*, heat, flame, fire: *ds.* **-e** 1115. < *swelan*, 'burn, be burnt up, in flame (a wound)'.

sweord, *n.a-stem*; SWORD: *gs.* **-es** 1106; *ds.* **swurde** 13; *dp.* **sweordum** 39V; *ap.* **sword** 15. See **sweord-bealo, -lēoma.**

‡**sweord-bealo**, *n.wa-stem*; SWORD-BALE, -evil, -death: *ns.* 1147. See **sweord, sweord-lēoma, morðor-bealo.** 2P.

‡**sweord-lēoma**, *m.n-stem*, [LEAM]; SWORD-light, flashing: *ns.* **swurd-lēoma** 35. See **sweord, hilde-lēoma.** NP.

swēte, *adj.*; SWEET, pure, pleasant, dear, fresh: *asm.* **swētne** 39V.

swilce, see **swylce.**

swīn, *n.a-stem*; SWINE, boar, (‡) boar-image: *ns.* **swȳn** 1111. See *Buf* 1286b *swīn ofer helme* 'boar atop the helmet', and 303b-04a *Eoforlīc scionon/ ofer hlēor-bergan* 'Boar-images shone/over the cheek-guards'; cp. the Sutton Hoo helmet (Bruce-Mitford [251] 27-8 and plate 16).

****swinsað**, *m.ua-stem?*, cry, noise: *as.?* 5V. TrF coined on the model of *fiscað* and *huntað* 'fishing' and 'hunting'; see Cmb 574.6.

swīðe, *adv.*, [SWITH]; much, very, very much: 1092; *comp.* more, rather: **swīðor** 1139.

sword, swurde, swurd-, see **sweord.**

swylc, *rel.pron.*; SUCH as, which: *apm.* **swylce** 1156; *adv.*, likewise, also: 41V, 1146, 1152: *conj.*, such as, as if: 36.

swȳn, see **swīn.**

swȳðan, *wv.(1b)*, or *v.(1)?*, [SWITH?]; strengthen, establish, support, use force against, affirm

(?): *inf.* 1106V. See Hlt 3-5 and his [888] 130.

sylf, see **self.**

syngāles, see **singāla.**

syrce, *f.n-stem*, [SARK]; shirt, corselet, mail-coat: *ns.* 1111.

syððan, see **siððan.**

****syððan**, *v.(2)?*, avenge?, atone?: *inf.* 1106V. The meaning 'avenge' is based on *Gen* 1525, *seðe*, now usually emended to *sēce* 'I shall seek'; see *Sprachschatz* (1st ed., 1864) II, 423. 'Atone' is based on *sēoðan*, 'boil, brood, afflict, disturb'; see Kock [1096] 109, Malone [1338] 266.

T

getēon, *v.(2)*, [TOW?, TUG]; draw, pull, withdraw, produce, restrain: *pret.3p.* **getugon** 15. See **þurh-tēon.**

tō, *prep.*, *w.dat.*; TO, toward, about: 14, 20, 27, 1119, 1138, 1139, 1154, 1158, 1159.

-torht, see **wuldor-torht.**

‡**torn-gemōt**, *n.a-stem.* [MOOT]; anger-meeting, battle?: *as.* 1140. *Torn* = anger, grief, misery, suffering, pain; *adj.*, bitter, cruel, grievous. *Gemōt* = society, assembly, court, council. NP.

trēow, *f.wō-stem*, [TRUCE]; fidelity, faith, trust, belief, pledge, agreement, treaty, grace, favour, kindness: *as.* **-e** 1072.

getruwian, *wv.(2,3)*, *w.acc.*, [I-TREOWE, TROW]; confirm, conclude; *pret.3p.* **getruwedon** 1095.

twā, *num.*; TWO: *afp.* 1095.

Þ

þā, *adv.*, [THO]; then, thereupon: 2, 9V, 13, 14, 18, 28, 43, 46, 1095, 1144; *conj.*, when, since, as: 1068, 1078, 1103, 1127, 1136, 1151.

þā, þām, þāra, þǣm, see sē.

þǣr, dem.adv.; THERE, then: (þēr)
7V, 1063, 1099, 1123; conj.,
where, when, as: 1079.

þǣra, þǣre, þǣs, see sē.

þæt, conj.; THAT, provided that, in
order that: 19, 44, 1075, 1082,
1086, 1087, 1098, 1099, 1141.
Abbreviated þ except 19, 44, 1082.

þē, rel.pron., [THE]; who, which,
what, on which: 1130; þē 9,
1123, 1135.

þē, see þū.

þēah, conj., usually w.opt.; THOUGH:
1102, 1130.

‡geþearfian, wv.(2). [THARF];
necessitate, impose necessity: pp.
geþearfod 1103.

þegn, m.a-stem, [THANE]; servant,
retainer, follower, freeman, cour-
tier; (†)warrior, hero: ns. þegn
13; ds. þegne 1085; gp. þegna
1085V; ap. -as 1081.

-þelu, see buruh-þelu.

þencan, wv.(1c); THINK, imagine,
consider, remember, intend,
learn, desire: pret.3s. þōhte 1139.

þēoden, m.a-stem, [THEDE?]; chief,
lord, prince, king: gs. þēodnes
1085. See þēoden-lēas.

‡þēoden-lēas, adj., [THEDE?];
lord-LESS: npm. -e 1103. See
þēoden. NP.

þēr, see þǣr.

þes, dem.pron. or adj.; THIS: nsm. 7;
nsn. þis 3; gsf. þisse 4; asm. þisne
9.

þindan, v.(3), swell, melt, pass
away, be angry: imp.p. -að 12V.
Mak and Rieger [1709] 10 =
swell (with courage), show your
temper, show your courage.

þis, þisne, þisse, see þes.

þōhte, see þencan.

þonne, adv.; THEN, further, there-
fore, however: 1104, 1106; conj.;

THAN, when, whenever: 40, 1066,
1121, 1139, 1143.

þorfte, see þurfan.

þū, pron.; THOU, you: ns. 27; ds. þē
26.

þurfan, prp.v.(3), [THARF]; need,
be required, must, have occasion
to, want, owe, have reason to:
pret.3s. þorfte 1071.

þurh, prep., w.acc.; THROUGH, from,
because of, with, by means of,
with a view to: 1101. See þurh-
tēon.

þurh-tēon, v.(2), [THROUGH +
TOW?, TUG]; bring about, effect,
finish, fulfil, draw, drag, con-
tinue, afford, undergo, inf. 1140.
DbB 178 'carry through (to its
conclusion)'. See þurh, getēon.
NP.

þȳrl, adj., [THIRL]; pierced, per-
forated, full of holes: nsm. 45,
þȳrel 45V.

U

*un-blinn, adj., [UN- + BLIN?];
incessant: dsn. -e 1097V. ? <
‡unblinnenlīce 'incessantly' in Bede
I, 6, p. 34, line 6, Miller ed.
(EETS, OS 95) or ? < blinn,
'cessation'; see Ele 825 blǣd
būtan blinne 'fame without ceas-
ing'.

un-dearninga, adv., [UN- +
DERN]; without concealment,
openly: 22. < dearnunga, adv.,
secretly, privately, insidiously.

under, prep., w.dat. of rest, acc. of
motion; UNDER, at the lower part
of; 8, 1078.

‡unflitme, adj.?. [UN-? + FLITE?];
(meaning unknown), undis-
puted?. or adv.?, unreservedly?,
indisputably?: dsn.? 1097; dsm.?
1129V; isn.? unflitne 1097V.
Most eds. < flītan 'strive, con-

tend', but Grienberger [682] 748 < *flēotan* 'float' = 'firmly, inviolably'. See **unhlitme, ellen.**

‡**unhlitme,** *adv.*?, [UN-? + LOT?]; (meaning unknown), very unhappily?, involuntarily?, without casting of lots? (*i.e.*, not by chance) 1129; **unhlytme** 1097V. See Introduction, p. 26 and **unflitme.**

un-hrōr, *adj.*, [UN- + ROAR?]; not strong, weak, useless: *nsn.* 45V. See **hrōr.**

un-slāw, *adj.*, [UN-]; not SLOW, active: *dsn.* -e 1097V. Cp. *Glc* 950 *elne unslāwe* 'active courage'.

‡**un-synnum,** *adv.*, [UN- + SIN]; guiltlessly: 1072.< *dp.* of *synn.*, 'sin, crime, hostility'.

ūs, see **ic.**

W

-walda, see **Folcwalda.**
wand, see **windan.**
wandrian, *wv.*(*2*); WANDER, roam, fly round, circle, hover, change, stray, err: *pret.3s.* **wandrode** 34. See **wundrian.**

‡**waðol,** *adj.*?, (meaning unknown): *nsn.*? 8. Mak, = wandering, < †*wāð*, 'wandering, journey, pursuit, hunt, flight'. Holthausen and Schücking, = *m.*, 'full moon'; Boer [141] 143, 'inconstant'; Grienberger [680] 100, 'half-covered'. MHG. *wadel* 'wandering, erratic' is often cited, referring to full or new moon.

†**wæfre,** *adj.*, unstable, wavering, wandering, restless, flickering, expiring: *nsn.* 1150.

wæg, *m.a-stem*; WAY, direction, path, journey, course of action: *as.* 43. Here adverbial phrase, *on wæg* 'away'.

wæl, *n.a-stem*, [WAL]; slaughter, carnage, battlefield; (*pl.*) slaughtered-bodies, corpses?: *ds.* -e 1113. See **Frēs-wæl, wælfāg, wæl-fȳr, wæl-sliht.**

‡**wæl-fāg,** *adj.*, [WAL + FAW, FOE?]; slaughter-stained: *asm.* -ne 1128. Other meanings suggested: 'blood-stained, deadlyhostile, forbidding', or < *wæl-*, 'water-, deep-pool-, stream-' = 'hostile to moving waters, marked by battling waters'. Perhaps an intentional pun: *wæl-fāg* 'slaughter-stained' and *wæl-fāg* 'water (*i.e.*, ocean)-hostile', both appropriate for this particular winter. See **swāt-fāh** (for a discussion of *fāg*), **wæl, wæl-fȳr, wæl-sliht.** Cp. *Bwf* 1631 *wæter under wolcnum, wæl-drēore fāg* 'water under the clouds, spotted with slaughterblood', and the same pun in *Gen* 1301a *wæl-strēamas* '-streams' and 1350a *wæll-regn* '-rain'. NP.

‡**wæl-fȳr,** *n.a-stem*, [WAL]; slaughter-FIRE, funeral fire: *gp.* -a 1119. Not 'funeral pyre' as in HMD 393. See **wæl, wæl-fāh, wælsliht.** NP.

wæl-sliht, *m.i-stem*, [WAL + SLEIGHT]; slaughter-stroke: *gp.* -a 28. *Sliht* = stroke, slaughter, murder, death, animals to be slaughtered. See **wæl, wæl-fāh. wæl-fȳr.** NP.

wære, wæron, wæs, see **eom.**

wǣr, *f.ō-stem*, [WARE]; treaty, agreement, faith, fidelity, protection, bond of friendship: *as.* -e 1100. See **frioðu-wǣr.**

wēa, *m.n-stem*; WOE, misfortune, evil, harm, trouble, grief, misery, sin, wickedness: *gp.* **wēana** 25, 1150. See **wēa-dǣd, wēa-lāf.**

†**wēa-dǣd,** *f.i-stem*; WOE-DEED, evil-
deed: *np.* -a 8. See **wēa, wēa-lāf.**
NP.

†**wēa-lāf,** *f.ō-stem*, [LAVE]; WOE-
remnant, survivors of a misfor-
tune: *as.* -e 1084, 1098. *Lāf* =
'what is left, remnant, legacy,
relic, remains, widow'. See **wēa,
wēa-dǣd.** NP.

weall, *m.a-stem*; WALL, stockade,
dike, earthwork, rampart, dam,
cliff: *ds.* -e 28V.

weallan, *rd.v.(7)*, [WALL]; WELL,
be agitated, rage, toss, bubble,
seethe, foam, be hot, boil, swarm,
flow, flood: *pret.3s.* **wēol** 1131.

wēana, see **wēa.**

weardian, *wv.(2)*, [WARD]; guard,
watch, protect, preserve, possess,
inhabit, rule, follow: *pret.3s.*
34V.

wearð, see **weorðan.**

weder, *n.a-stem*; WEATHER, air, sky,
breeze, storm: *np.* 1136.

wennan, *wv.(1a)*, [WEAN]; accus-
tom, inure, train, entertain,
treat, tame, wean: *pret.opt.3s.*
wenede 1091.

wēol, see **weallan.**

weorc, *n.a-stem*; WORK, labour,
action, deed, exercise, affliction,
suffering, pain, trouble, forti-
fication: *dp.* **worcum** 1100.

weorod-rǣden, *f.iō-stem*, [WERED
+ REDE]; troop-service, conditions
of military service: *as.* -e 1142V.
Cp. *Wld* I, 22 *wīgrǣdenne*, 'battle-
plan?, battle'. See **weorod-
rǣdend, worold-rǣdend, -rǣ-
denn, wrāð-rǣden.** NP.

weorod-rǣdend, *m.nd-stem*,
[WERED + REDE]; troop- or host-
prince, king: *ds.* -e 1142V. Refers
to Hengest. See **weorod-rǣden,
worold-rǣdend, -rǣden.** NP.

weorðan, *v.(3)*, [WORTH]; become,

get, be *(passive auxiliary)*, hap-
pen, arise, settle: *pret.3s.* **wearð**
1072.

weorðian, *wv.(2)*, [WORTH]; es-
teem, honour, worship, exalt,
praise, adorn, enrich, reward:
opt.3s. **weorðode** 1090.

weorðlice, *adv.,* [WORTHLY];
worthily, splendidly: *comp.* **wurð-
licor** 37. < *weorðlic, adj.,* 'im-
portant, valuable, splendid,
worthy, honourable, exalted, fit'.

weotena, see **wita.**

weotian, *wv.(2)*, [cp. WIT]; ap-
point, ordain, assure, destine:
pp. **witod** 26, (here) 'fated'.

wer, *m.a-stem*, [WERE]; male-being,
man, husband, (†)hero: *gp.* -a
37.

wesað, see **eom.**

wīc, *n.a-stem, or f.ō-stem,* [WICK];
dwelling-place, lodging, house,
village, street, bay; *(pl.)* camp,
fortress: *gp.* -a 1125.

wīde, *adv.,* [WIDE]; widely, afar,
far and wide: 25.

wīf, *n.a-stem*; female, lady, WIFE,
woman: *as.* 1158.

wīg, *n.a-stem,* [WI]; strife, contest,
war, battle, valour, army: *ns.*
1080; *ds.* -e 1084; *as.* 1083. See
wīgend.

†**wīgend,** *m.nd-stem,* [WYE]; war-
rior, fighter; *np.* 47, 1125; *vp.* 10.
See **wīg, rond-wīgend.**

wiht, *fn.i-stem,* [WIGHT]; person,
creature, being, thing, something,
anything, bit: *adverbially, as.*
1083b, 1083aV.

willan, *anom.v.*; WILL, be willing,
wish, desire, be used to, be about
to: *pres.3p.* **willað** 9; *opt.?* or
pret.3s. **wolde** 21, 1094; *opt.2s.*
wylle 27.

wind, *m.a-stem*; WIND: *ds.* -e 1132.

windan, *v.(3)*; *(tr.)* WIND, plait,

curl, twist, unwind, whirl, brandish, swing; (*intr.*) turn, fly, leap, start, roll, slip, go, delay, roll up, repair: *imp.p.* **windað** 12; *pret.3s.* **wand** 1119.

winnan, *v.(3)*, [WIN]; labour, resist, contradict, oppose, fight, struggle, rage: *imp.p.* **winnað** 12V; *pret.3s.* **won** 1132.

winter, *mn.ua-stem*; WINTER, (*pl.*) year: *ns.* 1132, 1136; *as.* 1128.

-wisa, see **hilde-wisa**.

wita, *m.n-stem*, [WITE]; counsellor, wise man, philosopher, witness, accomplice: *gp.* **weotena** 1098. < *witan*, 'know', *hence literally* 'a knower'.

gewitan, *v.(1)*, [I-WITE]; depart, go, pass away, die: *pret.3s.* **gewāt** 43; *pret.3p.* **gewiton** 1125.

witod, see **weotian**.

wið, *prep.*; (*w. acc.*) WITH, by, near, against, beside, at, through; (*w.dat.*) from, with (opposition), in return for, beside, near, opposite; (*w.gen.*) toward, to, at, against: 1083V, 1088, 1132.

wolcen, *n.a-stem*, [WELKIN]; lump, ball, cloud, sky, heavens: *dp.* **wolcnum** 8, 1119.

wolde, see **willan**.

won, see **winnan**.

worcum, see **weorc**.

word, *n.a-stem*; WORD, speech, sentence, statement, command, report, fame, promise: *dp.* **-um** 1100.

worod-, see **weorod-**.

worold, *f.ō-stem*; WORLD: *gs.* **-e** 1080. See **worold-rǣdend, -rǣden**.

‡**worold-rǣden,** *f.jō-stem*, [REDE?]; WORLD-custom or -law, 'obligation by custom' (DbB), 'universal obligation' (*i.e.*, revenge, Wms 93–6), 'worldly duty' (LwF

418): *gs.* **-ne** 1142. Malone [1363] 335 f., variant form of *worold-rǣdend*, qv. See Brd 313–30, and **worold, worold-rǣdend, weorod-rǣdend, -rǣden, wrāð-rǣden**. NP.

*****worold-rǣdend,** *m.nd-stem*, [WORLD + REDE]; earthly-ruler, king, lord, prince: *ds.* **-e** 1142V. Malone [1353] 22 and [1326] 159, interprets as Hnæf. See **weorod-rǣdend, -rǣden, worold, worold-rǣden**. NP.

-wracu, see **gyrn-wracu**.

*****wrāð-rǣden,** *f.jō-stem*, [WROTH + REDE?]; hostile-duty?, assistance, support: *gs.* **-ne** 1142V. See **weorod-, worold-rǣden**.

wrecan, *v.(5)*, [WREAK]; drive, advance, fulfil, utter, recite, expel, banish, persecute: *pp.* **wrecen** 1065.

wrecca, *m.n-stem*; WRETCH, fugitive, outcast, exile, adventurer, stranger, hero: *ns.* 25V, 1137, **wreccea** 25, *gp.* **wreccena** 25V.

wrecen, see **wrecan**.

-wudu, see **gomen-, gūð-wudu**.

†**wuldor-torht,** *adj.*, [WULDER + TORHT]; gloriously-bright: *npn.* **-an** 1136. *Wuldor*, 'glory, splendour, honour, praise, thanks, heaven'; *torht, adj.*, 'bright, radiant, beautiful, splendid, noble, illustrious'. NP.

wund, *adj.*, [WOUND]; wounded, sore: *nsm.* 43; *npm.* **-e** 1075.

wund, *f.ō-stem*; WOUND, sore, ulcer, wounding, injury: *dp.* **-um** 1113; *ap.* **-a** 47.

wundrian, *wv.(2)*, *w.gen.*; WONDER, be astonished, admire: *pret.3s.* **wundrode** 34V. See **wandrian**.

wunian, *wv.(2)*, [WON]; inhabit, dwell, exist, abide, be used to: *pret.3s.* **wunode** 1128.

Y

wurðlicor, see **weorðlice.**

wylle, see **willan.**

wynn, *f. jō-stem,* [WIN]; joy, rapture, pleasure, delight, gladness: *as.* **-e** 1080.

ymbe, *prep., w.acc. of place,* [EMBE, UMBE]; around, about, at, upon, near, along, 33.

ȳð, *f. jō-stem,* [YTHE]; wave, billow, flood; (†)sea, liquid, water: *ap.* **-e** 1132.

NAMES*

Dene, *m.pl.*, Danes: *dp.* **Denum** 1158; *ap.* 1090. See map, **Gūð-dene, Healf-dene, Scyldingas.**

Ēaha, *m.*, *a Danish warrior*: *ns.* 15, **Eahha** 15V. Mlr 86 objects to intervocalic *h* and emends to **Ēawa** (attested in *ASC* A716, A757), but Dkn cites *Echha* (*Liber Vitæ* 94, 96, ed. H. Sweet, *Oldest English Texts* [EETS OS 83] 156), **Æhcha** (charter of Wihtred, ed. Sweet, 428), and *Acha* (Bede, III, 6, p. 139). See also Bgg 25. (1).

Ēawa, see **Ēaha.**

Ēotan, *m.pl.*, Jutes: *gp.* **Ēotena** 1072V, 1088V, 1141V; *dp.* **Ēotenum** 1145V. Alternatively called *Euts*, WS. *Ȳte*, Anglian *Īuti* > *Ēote*, sometimes *Īutæ*. Originally from Jutland, they probably migrated near the Frisians, where they fell under Frisian hegemony. Some commentators believe *Ēotan* is an alternate name for the Frisians. See map, **eoten,** and MlW 215–16.

Finn, *m.*, *king of East Frisia*: *ns.* **Fin** 1096, 1152; *gs.* **-es** 36V, 1068, 1081, 1156; *ds.* **-e** 1128; *as.* **Fin** 1146. Son of Folcwalda and husband of Hildeburh. Cp. *Wds* 27 *Fin Folcwalding Frēsna cynne* 'Finn, son of Folcwalda,

[ruled] the race of the Frisians'. See MlW 150 and **Finns-burh.** (2).

Finns-burh, *f.*, Finn's-fortress: *ns.* **Finns-buruh** 36, **Finnes-burh** 36V. See **Finn, burh.**

Folc-walda, *m.*, Folk-Ruler, *father of Finn*: *gs.* **-an** 1089. Cp. *Bwf* 2595 *sē ðe ǣr folce weold* 'he who before ruled the people'. Chb 200 suggests *Folcwalda* is a title, the actual name being *Gōdwulf*. See MlW 150. NP. (3).

Frēsan, *m.pl.*, Frisians: *gp.* **Frēsena** 1093, **Frȳsna** 1104. Probably two tribes: the West Frisians lived west of the Zuider Zee, near Amsterdam; the East Frisians (evidently Finn's tribe), lived east and north of the Zuider Zee. See map, Chambers [315] 211, MlW 150–1, **Frēs-wæl,** and **Frȳs-land.**

Frēs-wæl, *n.*, Frisian-battlefield, *or* Frisian-slaughter: *ds.* **-e** 1070. Both meanings apply; the idea is 'on the Frisian battlefield', which was also a 'slaughter in Frisia'. See **Frēsan, wæl.**

Frȳs-land, *n.*, Friesland, Frisia: *as.* 1126. See **Frēsan, land.** NP.

Frȳsna, see **Frēsan.**

Gār-ulf, *m.*, (= *Gār-wulf*) Spear-Wolf, *a Frisian warrior*: *ns.* 18,

---

* I have glossed names literally, *e.g.*, Gārulf, 'Spear-Wolf'. However, Anglo-Saxon names need not necessarily mean anything, just as the modern name 'Frank Potter' does not indicate a candid ceramicist. Numbers in parentheses following personal name entries indicate total appearances in Searle's *Onomasticon Anglo-saxonicum*, giving some notion of the relative frequency of the name.

Gār-ulf—*contd.*

31; *ds.* **-e** 18V; *as.* 18V. Gārulf is son of Gūðlaf 33, and perhaps uncle or nephew of Gūðere; see Klaeber [1063] 307–8. Schneider [1811, 1813] and Beaty [78] [78] 372–3 cite Gārulf as Finn's son, and Chb 283–7 argues that Gārulf = Gefwulf (*Wds* 26), prince of the Jutes. See **gār.** 1P. (9).

Gūð-dene, *m.*, Battle-Dane: *ns.* or *np.* 18V. Bgg 25 = Sigeferð or the Danes; Jellinek [949] 428–9 = Hengest. See **gūð, Dene.** 1P.

Gūð-ere, *m.*, (= *Gūð-here*) Battle-Army, *a Frisian warrior*: *ns.* 18; *as.* or *ds.* 18V; *gs.* **Gūðheres** 33V. See discussion under **Gārulf,** also **gūð, gūð-here.** 1P. (3).

Gūð-lāf, *f.*, Battle-Remnant, -Survivor: *ns.* 16, 1148, referring to a Dane; *gs.* **-es** 33, a Frisian, father of Gārulf, See ChB 247 and **Gārulf, Gūðere, gūð, wēa-lāf.** 1P. (1).

Gūð-ulf, *m.*, (= *Gūð-wulf*) Battle-Wolf, *a Frisian warrior*: *gs.* 33V. Mlr tries to avoid the Gūðlāf problem by emending. See **gūð, Gārulf.** 1P. (1).

Healf-dene, *m.*, Half-Dane, *former king of the Danes, father of Hrōthgār*: *gs.* **-es** 1064, 1069V; *ūl.* = Half-Danes, *i.e., the tribe of Half-Dane*: *gp.* **-a** 1064V, 1069. See Malone [1320, 1337, 1402], TrF 11, and **Dene.** NP. (10).

Hengest, *m.* Stallion, Horse, *leader of the Danes after Hnæf's death*: *ns.* 1127; *gs.* **-es** 1091; *ds.* **-e** 1083, 1096. Perhaps the same person as Hengist, leader of the Saxon invaders of England; see Bede I, 15, and Malone [1338]. (3).

Here-Scylding, *m.*, Army-Scylding, *descendant of Scyld Scēfing or his tribe, the Danes*: *gp.* **-a** 1108. For Scyld Scēfing, see *Bwf* 1–52; see **Scyldingas.** 2P.

Hilde-burh, *f.*, Battle-Fortress, *daughter of Hōc, sister of Hnæf, wife of Finn*: *ns.* 1071, 1141. See **hild, burh.** 1P. (5).

Hnæf, *m.*, *prince of the Danes, son of Hōc, brother of Hildeburh. ns.* 2V, 1069; *gs.* **-es** 1114; *ds.* **-e** 40. See MlW 172. (2).

Hōc, *m.*, *a Dane?, father of Hildeburh and Hnæf*: *gs.* **-es** 1076. See MlW 172–3. (2, 6 variants).

Hrōð-gār, *m.*, Glory-, Victory-, *or* Joy-Spear, *current king of the Danes*: *gs.* **-es** 1066. *Hrōð-* < †*hrēð*, 'victory, glory', *or* < †*hrōðor*, 'joy, benefit, solace, pleasure'. See **gār.** BP. (3).

Hūn, *m.*, Giant?, High-One (= King)?, *a Dane?*: *ns.* 1143V. See **Hūnlāfing, Lāfing,** MlW 176, and Bgg 32–3. (7).

Hūn-lāfing, *m.*, Son-of-Hūnlāf, Kin-of-Hūnlāf, High-Remnant?, *probably a Dane*: *ns.* 1143. Sometimes taken as *as.* sword name; see Rieger [1708] 396 ff., Olrik [1587] 60 (p. 145 Hollander trans.), Koegel [1110] I, i, 167, Malone [1341] 300 ff. and [1326] 159, Hoops [896] 144 f. But R. Huchon, in *Revue Germanique*, 3 (1907) 626n, following Chadwick [303] 52n, cites Arngrímur Jónsson's summary of *Skjöldunga Saga*: Hunleifus, Oddleifus, and Gunnleifus (sons of Leifus, king of Denmark) = Hūnlāf, Ordlāf, and Guthlāf. For Arngrímur's text, see LwF 423–6 and Brd 330–55. See **Hūn, Lāfing.** NP. (1, Hūnlāf 7).

Lāfing, *m.*, Leaving, Remnant, *a sword name*: *as.* 1143V. The sword is a 'leaving' in the sense of being what remains when a file has done its work; cp. *Bwf* 1032 *fēla lāf* 'leaving of files' = sword. See **Hūn, Hūnlāfing.**

Ord-lāf, *m.*, Spearpoint-, Vanguard-Survivor, *or perhaps* Prince-Heir, *a Dane*: *ns.* 16. Probably same person as *Ōslāf* 1148. See **Hūnlāfing.** NP. (9).

Ōs-lāf, *m.*, God-Leaving?, *a Dane*: *ns.* 1148. Probably = Ordlāf 16. See **Hūnlāfing.** NP. (8).

Scyldingas, *m.pl.*, Scyld's-Descendants, *i.e., the Danes*: *gp.* **-a** 1069, 1154. See **Here-Scylding.**

Secgan, *m.*, *a Germanic tribe, evidently allied with the Danes*: *gp.* **Secgena** 24. Malone *ELH* 5 (1938) 65 locates them in northeastern Jutland near Aarhus. See map and **Sigeferð.**

Sige-ferð, *m.* or *f.*, Victory-Peace, -Protection, -Safety: *ns.* 15, 24. A Secgan warrior fighting with the Danes. Probably not the Sæferð of *Wds* 31 *Sǣferð Sycgum*; see MlW 193. NP. (Sige-frith 34).